Illustrator
Victoria Ponikvar Frazier

Editor
Karen J. Goldfluss, M.S. Ed.

Editorial Manager
Karen J. Goldfluss, M.S. Ed.

Editor in Chief
Sharon Coan, M.S. Ed.

Creative Director
Elayne Roberts

Cover Design
Denise Bauer

Art Coordinator
Cheri Macoubrie Wilson

Product Manager
Phil Garcia

Imaging
Ralph Olmedo, Jr.

Publishers
Rachelle Cracchiolo, M.S. Ed.
Mary Dupuy Smith, M.S. Ed.

S0-DVD-495

Math Snacks

Problem-Solving Fun with Food Manipulatives

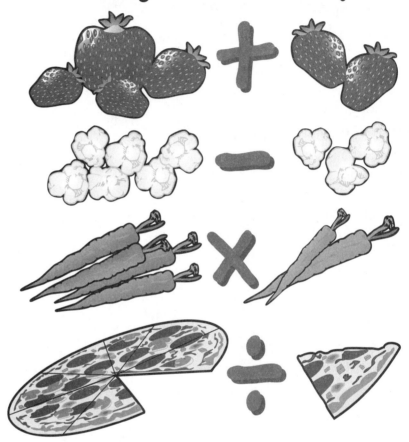

Author

Eliza Anne Sorte

Teacher Created Materials, Inc.
6421 Industry Way
Westminster, CA 92683
www.teachercreated.com
ISBN-1-57690-323-0
©1999 Teacher Created Materials, Inc.
Made in U.S.A.

Teacher Created Materials

Table of Contents

How to Use Math Snacks in Your Classroom

Introduction

What Is *Math Snacks*?

The enjoyment of a snack during a classroom break time is a familiar sight in most schools. The activities in *Math Snacks* provide teachers with a controlled way to introduce math concepts while making math time inviting, challenging, and fun. The methods used in this book help children make sense of mathematical concepts by allowing them to manipulate food items in order to solve problems. Careful observation of students as they work through the problem-solving process provides the teacher with a clearer picture of their mathematical thinking processes.

The activities in *Math Snacks* can be assigned at specific times of the year, or they can be used on a regular basis as extensions or reinforcement pages in an existing math program.

The Benefits of *Math Snacks*

The manipulative approach used in this unit has multiple benefits, the most important of which is the instant success students experience.

You can stretch the minds of the gifted students by asking them to solve their problems using a less familiar solution method. They can also work on giving clear, detailed solution sentences, or they can teach a younger student how to draw pictures or count to solve. Challenge students to use the writing process to create related problems for the snack being used. Even the students most difficult to manage are interested in the lesson when something worthwhile is being asked, solved, and ultimately eaten!

Success with this program can be measured in several ways. As students work through the problems, ask yourself these questions: Are students experiencing greater ease in finding solutions? Are they experimenting with a variety of problem-solving strategies? Are peer and teacher modeling an integral part of the problem-solving process? Are students challenged and motivated by the program? Are students actively involved in group discussions involving the solutions? Do students transfer the problem-solving techniques they learned in math to other areas of the curriculum? If your answer is yes to these questions, your students are already on the road to success.

Planning and Assessing with the Math Snacks Program

Planning for math snacks lessons requires a few simple steps. Before you begin the activities, send a letter to parents informing them about the program and how their children will participate. A sample letter is provided on page 10. Parent involvement is encouraged. The parent letter on page 11 outlines ways parents can become involved in their children's academic growth. Use the Math Snacks Planner (page 13) and the List of Potential Snacks (page 14) to organize each lesson and the materials you will need. Assessing your students' mastery of math concepts and understanding of problem-solving strategies can be achieved in several ways. Some of these methods are outlined on pages 15–18.

Introduction (cont.)

Using the Math Snacks Student Activities

There are 93 lessons in this book. The problem-solving activities provide reinforcement in the following math areas: patterning, addition, subtraction, multiplication, division, fractions, measurement, geometry, money, time, graphing, and estimation. Each activity lists the food item(s) you will need to solve the problem presented on the page. An activity may be completed individually by a student, as a group effort, or as a class endeavor. Adapt the lessons to meet your students' needs. Most of the lessons provide space for students to illustrate the problem and visualize ways to solve it. Once a picture or diagram has been drawn to show a possible solution, the student demonstrates an understanding of the problem and its solution by writing solution sentences and the number answer to the problem. Challenge activities which extend the problem-solving strategies are provided at the bottom of the student activity pages. Food items are not used with the challenge activities.

Decide in advance the most effective method for presenting the lesson. You may wish to present the snack, read the problem to the class first, and then distribute snacks and student activity sheets. Plan a procedure that works best for you and your students. It is important to note that not all students will write or draw something coherently or completely on their students pages. To assess their understanding and assist students with the problem-solving process, provide strategies and questioning techniques for solving problems. Suggestions are provided on pages 6–9.

The Blank Student Activity Form on page 12 can be used to create additional lessons for your students. Depending on your students' abilities, you may wish to have them use the form to write a problem for the class to solve. The Sample Parent Letter on page 10 suggests how parents can help their children complete this activity.

Students will handle food items as they complete the student activity lessons. Establish health and safety guidelines with your students before you begin the unit. Students should wash their hands before handling food items and place food on a clean surface such as a paper towel, etc. In addition to these precautions, be sure to check for any students who are allergic to the food items you will be using.

Using the Extensions, Tools, and Incentives

This section provides extension ideas, math manipulatives and charts that can be used to help students solve the activity page problems, incentive charts to plot students' progress through the lessons, and awards for a job well done. Reproduce pages as your students need them or copy the section and distribute it as a booklet for students to use throughout the unit.

Strategies Students Use to Problem Solve

Using *Math Snacks* as a supplement to your current math curriculum will increase the use of problem-solving skills in your students' daily work.

Some problems lend themselves to one particular strategy, while others can be solved in a variety of ways. Once students or groups of students become comfortable using one strategy, you may want to choose one of the following strategies to expand their strategy choices.

The following are methods that students may choose to solve the question for which they are seeking the answer.

❑ **Act It Out**

Students can use the problem like a script and act out the question. For example, they can actually hand out five candies to each person and see what happens.

❑ **Solve a Simpler Problem**

Students can use smaller numbers or a less demanding equation to figure out their solution. While recreating a problem, the student can look for number patterns.

❑ **Draw a Diagram**

Students can draw a representation of the problem to help them visualize the process for solving. This method seems to be the most common among primary students. Their diagrams may take the form of a circle with tallies, or they may be actual pictures of grapes being crossed out to show subtraction. Choose this method so they can see the relation between numbers and actual "things."

❑ **Make a Chart or Table**

Students can create tables or charts to organize the pictures or number information. Once they have the organization, the patterns they are seeking are sometimes more visible. Many students prefer a blank graph sheet to help them arrange their data. They may find it difficult to draw straight lines, so provide that paper for them if they need it.

❑ **Find a Pattern**

By using numbers on their papers or numbers on the hundreds chart, students can look for patterns to help them come up with the next logical number in a sequence or pattern.

Strategies Students Use to Problem Solve *(cont.)*

❑ **Make a Physical Model**

Students may need to use actual manipulatives to solve and work through their problem-solving processes. It is important to allow students to use whichever math tools they deem most beneficial. Sometimes, it is the actual snack that can help the students the most when they are allowed the chance to manipulate it.

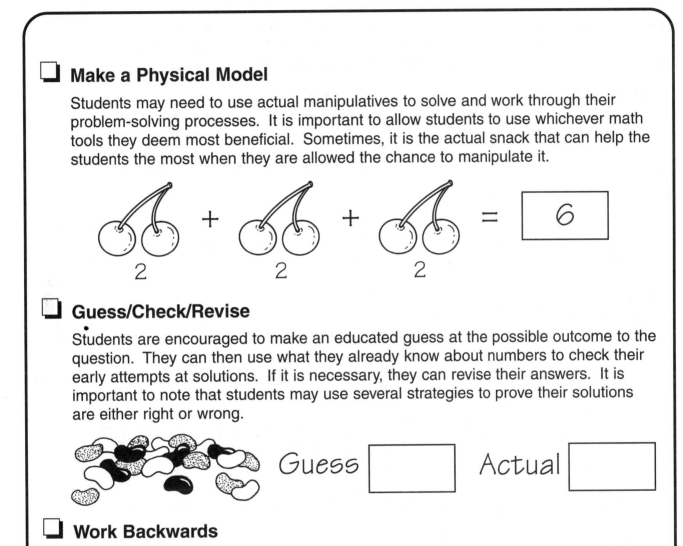

❑ **Guess/Check/Revise**

Students are encouraged to make an educated guess at the possible outcome to the question. They can then use what they already know about numbers to check their early attempts at solutions. If it is necessary, they can revise their answers. It is important to note that students may use several strategies to prove their solutions are either right or wrong.

❑ **Work Backwards**

Sometimes the answer is in front of the students, and they need to work their way backwards to find the final solution to the questions they are trying to answer. This is also a great technique to help students justify their answers by using a different strategy.

It is important that students have the opportunity to experiment with different strategies and that students are given the opportunity to communicate their efforts. Every student can express his or her thoughts about mathematics. Some students communicate with numbers, and others communicate with words. The important consideration here is that students develop more critical thinking skills and the ability to reach and explain a viable solution to any problem-solving situation. The activities in *Math Snacks* are designed to encourage this development.

Questions to Ask Students

The following are ideas on how to question your students while they are working through their *Math Snacks* problems. As you do more problem solving, these questions will flow naturally during your class discussions and can be applied in other content areas.

Helping Students to Work with One Another

"What do others think about what _____ said?"

"Would you ask the rest of the class that same question?"

"Do you understand what the rest of the group is saying?"

"Does anyone have the same answer but a different way to explain it?"

"What do you like about the way _____ solved the problem?"

Helping Students to Rely on Their Own Thinking

"Why do you think that?"

"How did you reach that answer?"

"Does that thinking make sense?"

"Can you make a model to prove that or write an equation to show that?"

"Why is that true?"

"Is there another way to solve that by using another strategy?"

Helping Students to Reason in Math

"Will that strategy work in all situations?"

"Does that always work?"

"Can you think of a problem this wouldn't work for?"

"Can you write a problem that will produce the same answers?"

8

Questions to Ask Students *(cont.)*

Helping Students to Learn to Invent and Solve Problems

"What would happen if we . . .?"

"What are some possibilities here?"

"Do you see a pattern?"

"What decision do you think he or she should make?"

"Can you continue a pattern?"

"How did you think about the problem?"

"How could you tell someone else to get started on a similar problem?"

"Can you predict the next one? What about the last one?"

Helping Students to Connect Math, Ideas, and Applications

"How does this relate to . . .?"

"What uses of math did you find in the newspaper?"

"How does your family use math every night?"

"Can you give me an example of . . .?"

"Where have we seen something similar to this solution?"

"What ideas have we learned that helped you solve this problem?"

"Have you solved a problem similar to this before? How was it the same? How was it different?"

These questions are just the beginning of the endless learning process that can go on when students are asked to think and, most importantly, explain their thinking. Have your students help you add to these lists as well as create new categories of questions for you and for their classmates.

Sample Parent Letter

Dear Parents,

Math is an essential part of our everyday lives. This year I hope to help your child see math in real world contexts. In order to do this, we will be using a variety of methods. One of these methods is called math snacks. We will be using food to make math motivating, fun, and educational.

In addition to the classroom activities provided in our math snacks program, your child will be creating a math problem for the rest of the class to solve. He or she will assume the role of teacher and present the problem to the class. The problem-solving activity requires the use of a snack to be supplied by the student teaching the activity. Please try to help your child choose a nutritious and inexpensive snack.

The problem your child creates should in some way relate to our class activities and the snack. Some of the math strands we will be covering are patterning, graphing, adding, subtracting, multiplying, dividing, fractions, geometry, time, money, and estimating. Problems can range anywhere from determining the cost of an item to how many of the item each student will receive.

Here are a few ideas to get your child thinking about his or her math problems:

Crackers Count—How many whole crackers will we need if each person in our class gets one half of a cracker?

Carrots—Estimate the length of your carrot in centimeters. Measure it and compare your estimate to the actual length.

If your child has any difficulty coming up with a snack or a problem, please do not hesitate to contact me. If you are unable to supply a snack for any reason, please let me know as soon as possible so other arrangements can be made.

Your child's snack day is _____ .

School Phone Number: _____

List your child's food allergies here, please. _____

Thank you for helping make math a real life experience.

Sincerely,

_____

Math Snacks at Home

Dear Parents,

This year we will be using food as one of many learning techniques in our classroom. One way we will be using snacks is to make math real to your child. We will be solving math problems by using food items as manipulatives. We will also discuss nutritional information, prices, measurements, and overall number sense as each of them relate to math and the real world. Listed below are ten activities you can do at home to encourage your child to think and reason mathematically in a real life setting.

1. Have your child organize measuring tools and containers in order, from largest to smallest and vice versa.

2. Have your child read a recipe to you as you do the day's cooking.

3. Have your child set the timer for your cooking and predict when the timer will go off on a real clock.

4. Have your child help you price items in a grocery store, looking in particular for the most expensive and least expensive items.

5. Have your child guess how much fruit weights before you actually weigh it. Depending on your child's level, you may want to have him or her estimate the cost of the fruit based on how much it does weigh.

6. Have your child write your shopping list, grouping the items you need by category. Again, depending on your child's level, you may want to create the categories and have your child match each item to those areas.

7. Have your child estimate how many items fit in different cup sizes. For example, ask your child to estimate how many chocolate chips fit in $\frac{1}{4}$ cup (60mL). Then, have him or her guess how many would be in $\frac{1}{2}$ cup (120mL), 1 cup (240 mL), etc.

8. Have your child look at the nutritional panel on cereals and other food packaging. Show him or her what one serving of the cereal looks like, how many calories it has, and how many grams of fat there are.

9. Have your child set the table. He or she will need to decide how many of each utensil is needed as well as plates, napkins, and cups. When finished, have your child count or mentally add the total number of items.

10. Overall, include your child in as many of the daily routines that involve math as possible. You will be surprised at how many little things in your daily life interest, entertain, and educate your child.

Thank you for making math an important part of your child's life. For more suggestions on how you can reinforce math concepts at home, please contact me at school.

Sincerely,

_____

Blank Student Activity Form

Food: _____

Problem: _____

_____

_____

Solution Sentences: _____

_____

_____

Number
Answer

Challenge: _____

_____

Math Snacks Planner

Depending on how you plan to acquire the various snacks, you may want to plan ahead which snacks you will need. Remember to incorporate these snack activities into special theme celebrations or holiday activities wherever possible. If you work in a team-teaching environment, take turns preparing the math snacks. Plan for the month which snacks you have on hand and/or need to acquire, which snacks meet theme needs, and who will do the actual organizing of the snacks and students' activity sheets. Below is a chart to help you look at the math snacks program in relation to your special classroom situation. If you are having students provide the snacks, you may want to include a students' name in each week's time frame.

Months	Snacks	Provider	Concept
August			
September			
October			
November			
December			
January			
February			
March			
April			
May			
June			
July			

Remember that these activities should be fun for all of those involved. Choose snacks and concepts that fit into your curriculum and are easy to provide, implement, manage, and assess.

List of Potential Snacks

Most snacks listed below can be purchased for under $4.00 per class serving. They may also, in most circumstances, be purchased in a generic brand.

These are just a few of the possible snacks available for class use. Snacks brought into the classroom for various celebrations also make good math snacks. Wherever possible, try to substitute sugar-free items for snacks traditionally made with sugar.

- alphabet-shaped cookies, cereals, or crackers
- animal-shaped crackers or cookies
- any flavor of homemade cookies and bars
- apples
- bananas
- boxed snacks
- bubble gum (sugar free)
- bulk trail mix (store bought or homemade)
- candies
- candy-coated chocolates (variety of colors)
- carrots
- cauliflower
- celery
- sugar wafers (variety of colors and sugar free, if possible)
- cherries
- chocolate bars
- chocolate-covered raisins or peanuts
- chocolate or butterscotch chips
- cold cereals
- cookies
- corn
- donut holes

- fortune cookies (with children's fortunes)
- fry bread
- geometrically-shaped crackers (square, triangle, circle, hexagon, star)
- grapes
- gummies (spiders, worms, bears, etc.)
- kiwi
- licorice (flavors, sizes, or textures)
- lifesavers (hard or chewy)
- marshmallows (small, large, or colored)
- noodles
- oranges
- peanuts
- peas in pods
- popcorn
- pretzel sticks
- pretzels
- raspberries
- rice
- rice cakes (mini or regular)
- strawberries
- string beans
- tortillas (flour or chips)
- yogurt-covered raisins or peanuts

Assessment

Assessing students' performance with this program can be done in numerous ways, depending on your established classroom grading policies. Making the assessment usable and manageable is essential. Whichever assessment is used, the students need to be made aware of what they are to demonstrate.

Listed below are additional assessment strategies you may wish to include. They can be used as described, or they can be slightly altered to meet your classroom needs.

The Thinking Process Method

The students' thinking strategy for problem solving is assessed. Determine the thinking process by assessing the work presented on paper either with pictures, numbers, or written explanations. Another approach is to ask questions about how a problem was solved and assess the accuracy of the student's response.

Space has been provided on the student activity pages for writing, drawing, supplying number answers, and answering challenge questions. Student responses in these areas can be used as part of your assessment process. For example, you can check a student's final number answer for accuracy and compare it to see if it matches the student's explanations or illustrations on the page. In addition to assessing the complete and descriptive explanation of the solution in sentence form, you may also want to give credit for verbal explanations given to you individually or in front of the class.

The Roster Method

Each child's name is listed in a roster format with squares available for check marks or numbers next to each name.

A check can be given for each part of the problem the student has completed. If the challenge is attempted, a "C" can be noted in a box or another check could be given. Another use of the roster list would be to give a numerical value for each part of the problem that is correct. For example, a student who successfully completes all three parts of a problem would receive a numerical value of $3/3$. If the challenge is attempted, a $4/3$ could be denoted or a plus sign could be added following the numbers. If a child provides a solution to the class, the checks or numbers can be circled to depict that. On the student's paper the grade for the problem can be marked with numbers or encouraging words.

The File Folder Method

In this method, a math snack anecdotal record folder is created. To do this, arrange large index cards, one on top of the other. Place tape along the upper edge of each index card. Then overlap the cards so that about $1/4$" (.6 cm) shows on the bottom of each card. This leaves just enough room to write each student's name. This can be done on both sides of the inside of the folder. The cards should flip easily up and down. You are now ready to record any student's vital strategy information.

Assessment *(cont.)*

The File Folder Method *(cont.)*

Record the date and whichever strategy the child used. Ask yourself the following questions:

- How does the student prefer to count?
- Can the student solve by using only equations?
- Can the student self-start, or does he or she require assistance?
- Is the student willing to share his or her solutions with the class?
- Are there consistent number reversals?
- Are the student's solution sentences complete and detailed?

These small bits of information will not only give you a look at each individual's needs but also the needs of the entire classroom. These details can help you choose upcoming math snacks or possible follow-up lessons. It is also adviseable to write, for your own records, on the outside of the folder the date, the snack used, and the mathematical focus.

The Sticky Note Method

While listening to students' sharing, quick notes can be taken on sticky notes which may later be added to a student math portfolio, rewritten for report cards, or added to an anecdotal notebook.

The Walk Around Method

During work time, quietly wander about the classroom and monitor the ongoing progress. At this time, you can stop and question students orally or jot down pertinent data for re-evaluation. Your evaluations can be written directly on their snack papers or on a separate piece of paper.

The Student Evaluation Method

In addition to your ongoing assessment, the students can also provide great insight into their mathematical accomplishments, disappointments, and needs. This can be done with the whole class, individually, on paper, or verbally. Students' feedback on their progress may be more interesting and beneficial than the observations you make.

By evaluating the results of one or all of the assessments, you can modify upcoming math snacks as well as other lessons. You can expand on favorite student foods or content areas. You can also review troubling areas or do a pretest for information that you will be covering. The various assessments also provide valuable dialogue for parent-teacher conferences. Often the students struggling with regular math routines will have unique and sometimes extremely successful problem-solving strategies. This can lead to a comfortable way to inform parents about the possibility of learning difficulties, while at the same time pointing out the positive attributes of their child's mathematical ability.

Student Assessment Roster

Student	Dates															

Student Evaluation

Name _____ Date _____

1. Why is math important? _____

_____

2. What makes math fun? _____

_____

3. What is your best problem-solving strategy? _____

_____

4. Which math snacks activity is your favorite and why? _____

_____

_____

5. What is one thing you have learned in math? _____

_____

6. What is one thing you would like to work harder on in math? _____

_____

7. What would you like to see added to our math snacks program? _____

_____

_____

8. List three snacks you would like us to have in our class.

_____

_____

_____

Student Activities

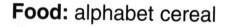

1

Awesome Alphabet

Food: alphabet cereal

Using your alphabet cereal letters, spell your name. Now, create your name in pattern form with your pencil.

Example: **E, L, I, Z, A, E, L, I, Z, A, E, L, I, Z, A, E, L, I, Z, A**

Show five other patterns by using any letters from your cereal. (Repeat each pattern three times.)

1. KYLIE

2. KYLIE

3.

4.

5.

Solution Sentences: _____

_____

_____

_____

Cereal Challenge: Whose name in the class would have the longest pattern?

Why? _____

_____

2

Animal Cracker Parade

Food: animal-shaped crackers

Choose two different animal crackers to arrange in the patterns below. You will need a few of each. In the space below each letter pattern, draw a picture of what the animal cracker pattern would look like. For a challenge, write the next three letters for each pattern.

A   B   A   B   A   B   ___   ___   ___

AA   BB   AA   BB   AA   BB   ___   ___   ___

A   BB   A   BB   A   BB   ___   ___   ___

A   B   A   BB   A   BBB   ___   ___   ___

Solution Sentences: Describe an ABAB pattern. _____

_____

_____

Cracker Challenge: Create your own animal pattern picture by using animal crackers from your parade. Remember to label the pattern.

Fresh Fruit Kabobs

Food: fresh fruit

For this activity you will need a kabob stick. Choose eight pieces (chunks) of fruit. Place the fruit on your kabob stick to make a pattern. Draw a picture of your kabob pattern and label it with pattern alphabet letters.

Solution Sentences: Write what the next eight pieces of fruit would be in your kabob pattern if you continued it.

_____

_____

_____

_____

_____

Kabob Challenge: If everyone in our class used eight pieces of fruit, how many pieces would we use in all?

Ten Teddy Bears

Food: teddy bear crackers or gummies (various flavors)

Lay out your 10 teddy bears on your desk. (You need at least two flavors or colors). In the space below, write down the pattern by using one letter for each different color. For example: B, C, B, C, B...

Rearrange your teddy bears and write down your new pattern by using the same alphabet letters for each color that you used in the above pattern.

Rearrange your teddy bears one more time in a different pattern and write that pattern down.

Solution Sentences: How can you prove each pattern of 10 teddy bears is different?

_____

_____

_____

Bear Challenge: If a small package of teddy bears cost $.45, how much would it cost to buy a package for each student in the classroom?

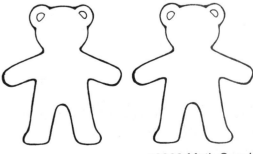

Creative Cereal Patterns

Food: cereal with shapes, raisins

Place two or three handfuls of cereal in a pile. Place one handful of raisins in another pile. Create an interesting pattern using the cereal. Draw your pattern on the left side of the space below.

Now combine the cereal and the raisins. Draw your pattern on the right side of the space below.

Solution Sentences: Which pattern was easier to create? Why?

_____

_____

_____

_____

Cereal Challenge: Each cup of cereal has 15 raisins in it. How many raisins would be in three cups?

6

Mouthwatering Watermelon

Food: watermelon slices

Today we have a huge watermelon to share with our class. Each of you will receive one slice of watermelon on a paper plate. Take all the seeds (dark and light) out of your watermelon slice. Separate the two kinds of seeds. Count each group. Draw a picture of the two groups of seeds. How many seeds are there in all?

Solution Sentences: _____

_____

_____

Number
Answer

Seedy Challenge: Work in a group with two other students. Find the total number of light and dark seeds you have. Write addition problems to show each.

Nubby Licorice Numbers

1

Food: small licorice pieces (two colors—red and black)

If each piece of red licorice is worth five points and each piece of black licorice is worth three points, how much is your cup of licorice worth? Draw a picture to show how you would solve this problem.

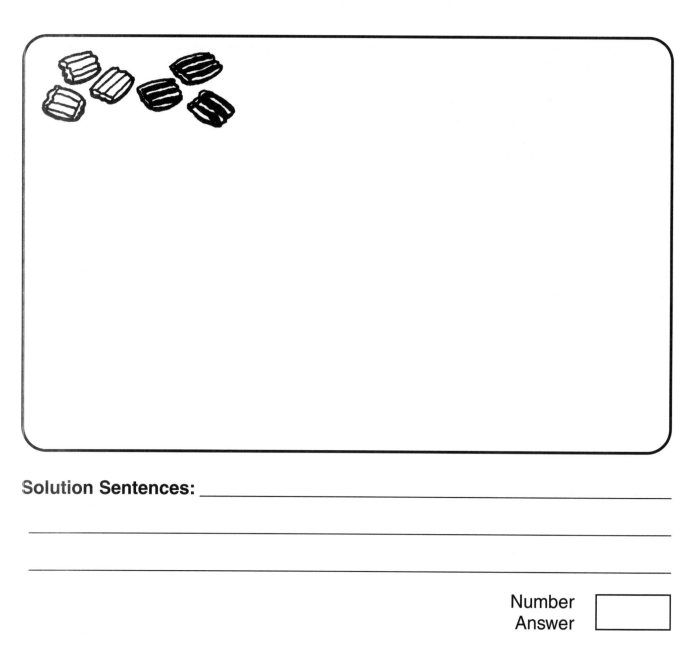

Solution Sentences: _____

_____

_____

Number
Answer

Counting Challenge: There were 42 pieces of licorice in each bag and there are two bags. How many pieces of licorice are there in all? How many pieces would there be in four bags?

Scrumptious S'mores

8

Food: chocolate bars, marshmallows, graham crackers

We will be making s'mores in our class today. You will need two halves of a graham cracker, one large marshmallow, and half a chocolate bar. If everyone needs the same ingredients, how many items do we need in all? Remember, each ingredient counts as one item. Draw a picture to show your ideas for solving this problem.

Solution Sentences: _____

_____

_____

Number
Answer [   ]

Chocolate Challenge: If everyone needed half a chocolate bar, how many whole chocolate bars were needed for our class?

Plentiful Pears

Food: pears

We have four large cans of pears today. Let's count the number of pears in each can. Use this information to show how many pear pieces we have in all. Draw your picture in the space below.

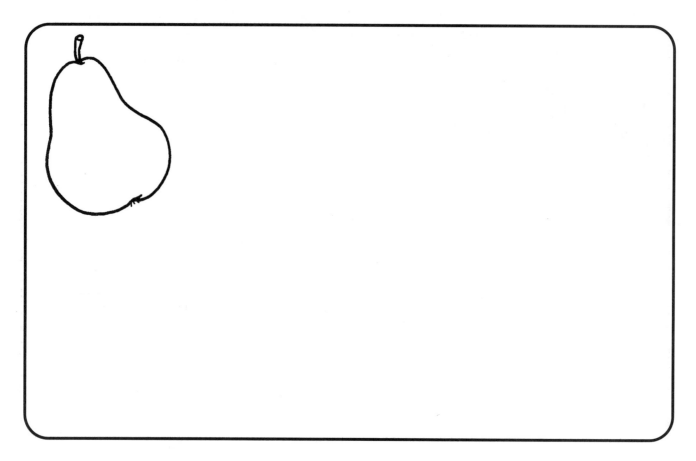

Solution Sentences: _____

_____

_____

Number
Answer [   ]

Chopped Challenge: One pear makes four slices. How many pears are needed to make the sixteen slices in our cans?

Crazy Celery

Food: celery sticks

We bought four bundles of celery. Each bundle has five long stalks of celery. Each stalk is nine inches (23 cm) long. In the box, draw a picture to show how long each bundle would be if we lined up the stalks end to end. How long would all four bundles be?

Solution Sentences: _____

_____

_____

Number
Answer

Celery Challenge: If each bundle weighed half a pound (225 g), how much did all four bundles weigh? If each pound costs $.80, how much did we pay for our celery?

Wonderful Wafers

11

Food: sugar wafers (three flavors—sugar free, if possible)

There are three flavors of wafers in our packages. There are 22 wafers of each flavor. Add all three rows and find the total number of wafers in a package. Draw a picture to show your addition.

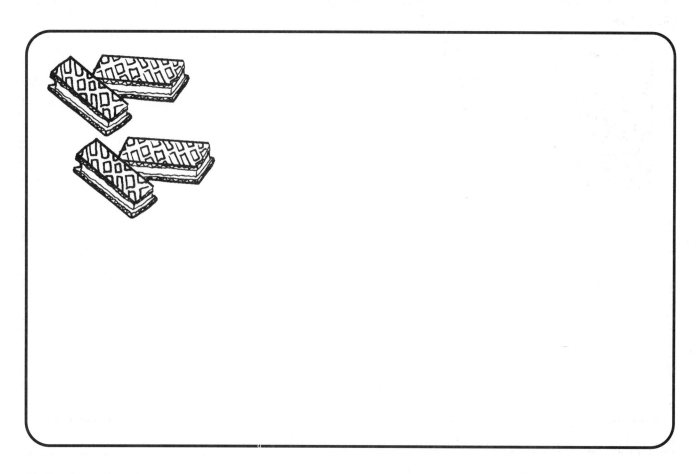

Solution Sentences: _____

_____

_____

Number
Answer [   ]

Counting Challenge: If there are 22 wafers in each row and there are three rows per package, how many wafers are there in five packages of wafers?

After Lunch Crunch

12

Food: trail mix (peanuts, almonds, raisins, candy-coated chocolates)

Trail mix makes a tasty snack. Make your trail mix with a small handful of each of these ingredients: peanuts, almonds, raisins, candy-coated chocolates. In the space below, draw the groups of each item you have in your trail mix. Then count the number of pieces of each item you have and solve for the total number of treats.

Solution Sentences: _____

_____

_____

Number
Answer

Crunchy Challenge: Write some story addition problems using the numbers of treats you have. Use the back of this paper to write your problems. Include number sentences to show the number answers for each.

For your second challenge, find out how many pieces you will have left if you eat half of them.

Pretzel Pickups

Food: pretzel sticks (snack-size packages)

Separate the pretzels into bundles of five. In the space below, show what your grouped pretzels look like. Now count by fives to find the total number of pretzels you have. Don't forget to add any loose pretzels you have left over.

Solution Sentences: _____

_____

_____

Number
Answer

Pretzel Challenge: Each package of pretzels costs 15 cents. If there are 10 packages in a box, how much does a box cost? If each small package contains 40 pretzels, how many pretzels are there in a box?

Birthday Cupcake Math

Food: any birthday cupcakes

Twenty-four cupcakes were made for the birthday party. If this was done three more times, how many cupcakes would we have in all? Show what this would look like in the space below.

Solution Sentences: _____

_____

_____

Number
Answer

Cupcake Challenge: We have 24 cupcakes. Each cupcake costs $.11. How much would they cost in all? (Try to solve by using your mental math.)

Candy Count

15

Food: individually wrapped candy pieces (sugar free, if possible)

There are two bags full of candy. The first bag holds 24 candies and the second bag holds 22 candies. How many candies are there in all? Draw a picture to show how you found your answer.

Solution Sentences: _____

_____

_____

Number
Answer _____

Candy Count Challenge: Do we have enough for our class today? If we do, how many candies will each person get, and how many will be left over?

Holiday Canes

16

Food: candy canes

As part of a store special, I found 55 cracked candy canes. I also found 36 whole candy canes. I decided to share the whole candy canes. If each of you receives one candy cane, how many whole candy canes will I have left? Draw a picture to show the candy cane subtraction.

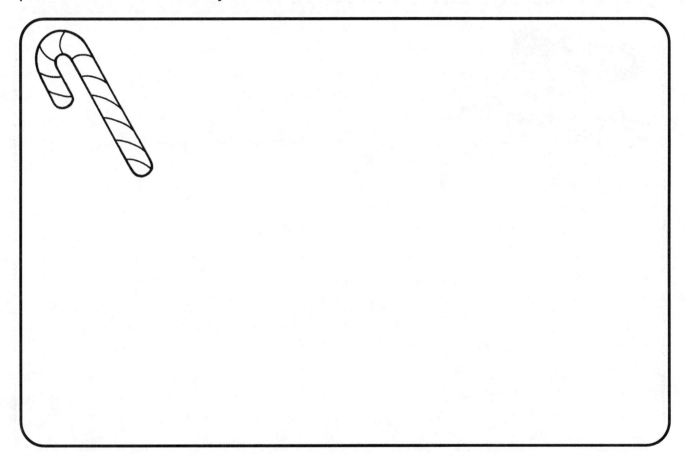

Solution Sentences: _____

_____

Number
Answer

Candy Cane Challenge: Each candy cane that was broken cost $.10. Each candy cane that was not broken cost $.15. Using the information above, how much did I spend for all of the candy canes I bought?

Creme-filled Subtraction

Food: vanilla creme cookies (sugar free, if possible)

Today I counted 75 cookies in one box! I decided we will use only 47 of them.
How many cookies will be left? Draw cookies to show how you would solve this
problem.

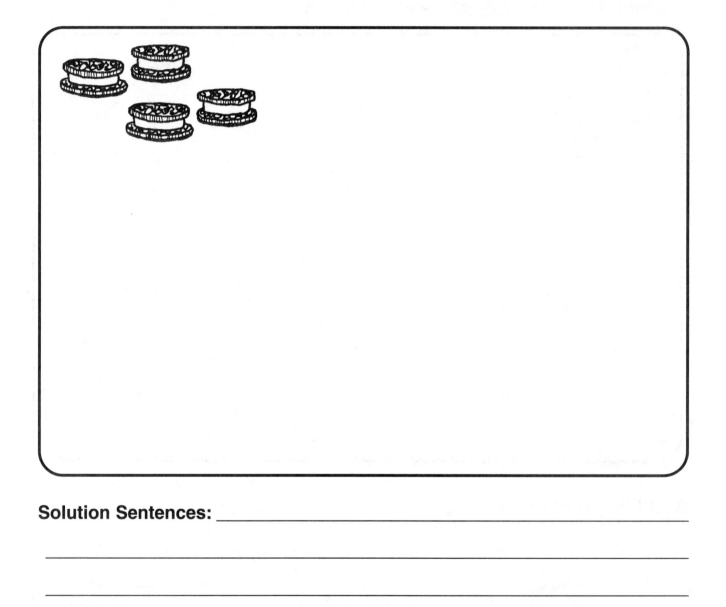

Solution Sentences: _____

_____

_____

Number
Answer [   ]

Cookie Challenge: The cookies were on sale. I spent a total of $4.80 on four
boxes of cookies. How much did each box of cookies cost?

Disappearing Apples

18

Food: apple slices

For our snack today we have 36 apple slices. How many apple slices will be left after each person in our class gets one apple slice? In the space below, show what this would look like.

Solution Sentences: _____

_____

X X X

Number Answer	

Chopped-Up Challenge: Each apple has been cut into four slices. How many apples were cut to get our 36 slices?

Buttercup Biscuits

Food: biscuits

We have 62 biscuits. I gave 24 to another class. I also gave six to the office staff. How many do I have left for us to use for our math snacks activity? In the space below, draw a picture to show how you would solve this problem.

Solution Sentences: _____

_____

_____

Number
Answer

Biscuit Challenge: If I had 62 whole biscuits and decided to cut each biscuit in half, how many biscuit halves would I make?

Cracker Shapes Count

Food: bite-size snack crackers (square, triangle, circle shapes)

From a large bowl containing mixed shapes of bite-size snack crackers, collect two or three handfuls of the crackers. Sort them by shape. In the space below, draw pictures to show how many there are of each cracker shape you collected.

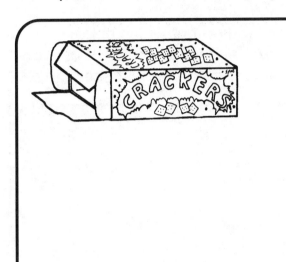

Solution Sentences: Which shape has the most crackers? How many more crackers does the largest cracker group have than the second largest group of crackers? How many more crackers are in the second largest group than are in the smallest group?

_____

_____

_____

_____

Cracker Challenge: Are there more or fewer crackers in the largest cracker group than in the second and third groups combined? On the back of this paper, write a number sentence to show how many more or fewer.

Fruit Snack Subtraction

Food: bite-size fruit snacks (packaged for individual servings, with color variety)

What is the total number of fruit snacks in your package? Draw a picture showing how many of each color you have in your package. Arrange your snacks according to your picture grouping. Count to find out which color represents the group with the most snacks. Count to find out which color represents the group with the fewest snacks. How many more snacks must you add to make the smallest snack pile equal the number in the largest snack pile?

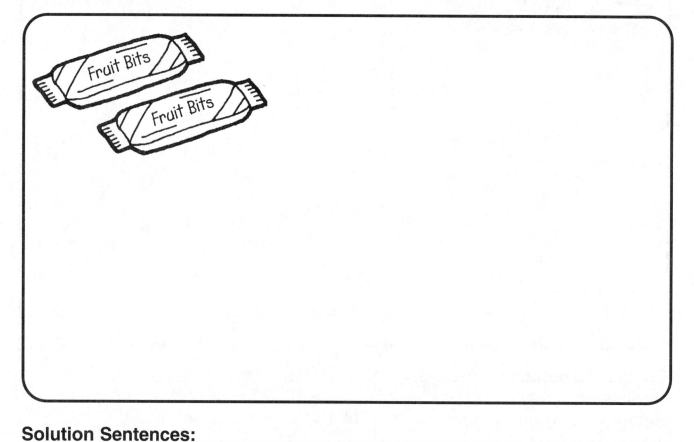

Solution Sentences: _____

_____

_____

Number
Answer

Fruity Challenge: Get together with two other students and compare the numbers and colors of fruit snacks you each have in your packages. Decide who has more of each color and what the difference is for each color.

Strawberry Stumper

Food: strawberries

There are 58 strawberries in one crate. If I give 22 to another class and keep the rest for our class, how many have I kept for us? Draw a picture to show the subtraction.

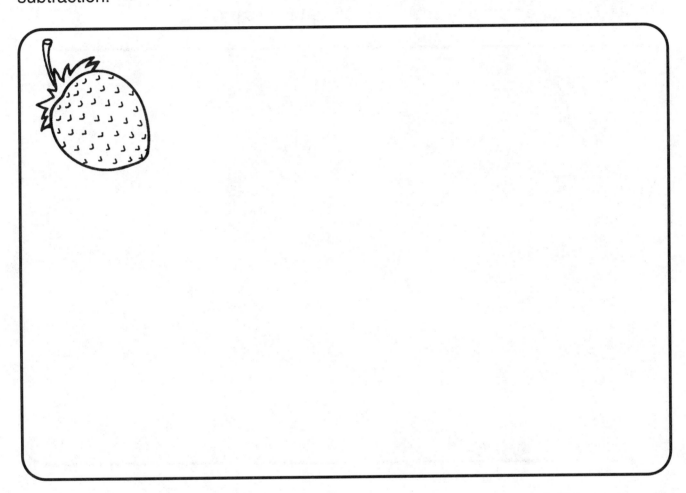

Solution Sentences: _____

_____

_____

Number
Answer

Strawberry Challenge: One crate of strawberries takes 45 minutes to clean and fill. How long would it take to fill six crates with clean strawberries?

Cherry Shopping

Food: cherries

After shopping I was so hungry that I ate seven cherries from a bunch I had just purchased. On the way home, five cherries fell out of the bag. If there were 56 cherries in the bunch I originally purchased, how many were now left to share with you? Draw a picture to show the solution to this problem.

Solution Sentences: _____

_____

_____

Number
Answer [   ]

Cherry Challenge: If there are 15 trees in each row and each orchard has 10 rows, how many cherry trees are there in all?

Pumpkin Seed Problems

Food: roasted pumpkin seeds (about 2 cups/250 grams of seeds per group of three students)

Get together with two students. Spread the pumpkin seeds on some paper towels. Find a way to hand out the same number of seeds to each student in your group. If you have any seeds left over, put them aside. How many seeds did each of you get? Show what this looks like in the space below.

Solution Sentences: _____

_____

_____

Number
Answer [   ]

Pumpkin Seed Challenge: How many seeds would be left over if each group member received only five seeds each?

Great Grapes

Food: grapes

I bought a few bunches of grapes. The total number of grapes is 75. I was hungry and ate 36 of them. How many grapes are left? In the box, draw a picture to show the grape subtraction.

Solution Sentences: _____

_____

_____

Number
Answer

Bunchy Challenge: We have 39 grapes to share with our class. How many grapes can each person have so that everyone has an equal number? How many will be left over?

Friendly Fruit Bars

Food: fruit bars

If there were 40 fruit bars in a carton and we each had one fruit bar, how many bars would we have left? Draw a picture to show the subtraction in this problem.

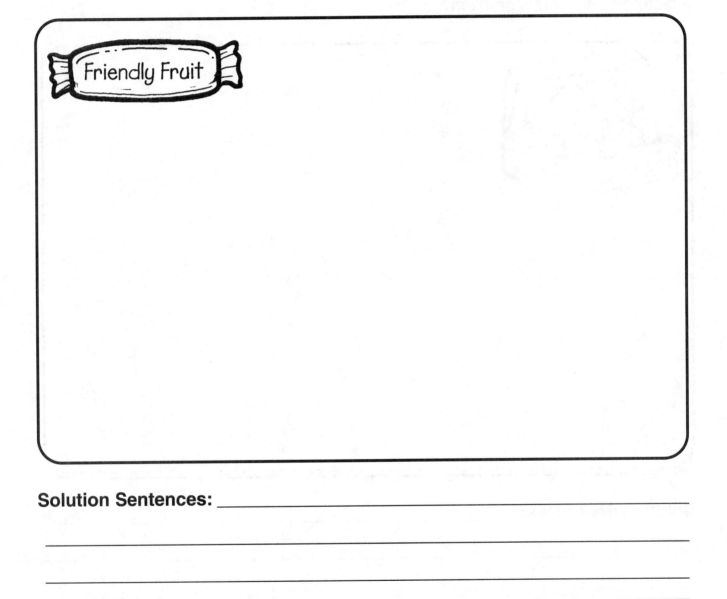

Solution Sentences: _____

_____

Number
Answer

Fruit Bar Challenge: If we cut the original bars in half and give each student in the class one of the halves, how many bars would we have left? Would there be enough of the remaining bars for each student to receive another half bar? Why or why not?

Donut Hole Subtraction

Food: donut holes

We have four dozen donut holes to share in class. If each student, the teacher, and the principal share our treat, how many donut holes will be left over? Draw a picture to show this problem.

Solution Sentences: _____

_____

_____

Number
Answer ☐

Donut Challenge: How many dozen donut holes would we have to buy for each student in the class to receive three donut holes? How many donut holes would be left over?

Multiplying Muffins

Food: muffins (any variety)

Yummy! I bought two boxes of muffins fresh from the bakery. In each box there are six muffins in each row and there are three rows. In the space below, show what the box of muffins looks like. How many muffins did I buy in all?

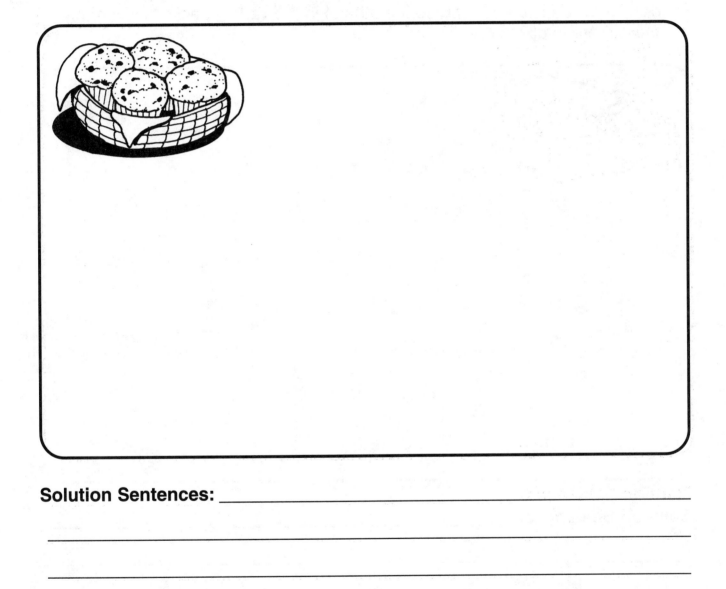

Solution Sentences: _____

_____

_____

Number
Answer [   ]

Cooking Challenge: The baker said that the muffins had been out of the oven for only 15 minutes. She said this at 1:00 p.m. What time did she take them out of the oven?

29

Snack Pack Multiplication

Food: two boxes of individually packaged snack bags (chips, popcorn, etc.)

Today we have two boxes of individual snack bags. For each box count the number of bags in each row and the number of rows in the variety pack box of snacks. Draw a picture to represent the bags in the variety packs. How many bags are there in all?

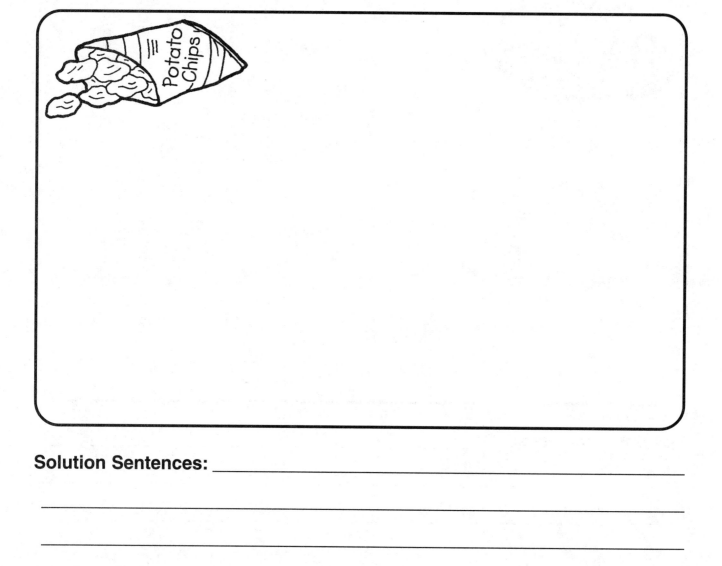

Solution Sentences: _____

_____

_____

Number
Answer

Snack Pack Challenge: How many bags will be left if each person in our class gets one snack bag? What could we do with the leftovers?

Raisin Snowmen

Food: yogurt-covered raisins

If each student in the class uses three yogurt-covered raisins to make a snowman and each student makes five snowmen, how many yogurt-covered raisins would we need for our class? Draw a picture to show how this multiplication problem can be shown.

Solution Sentences: _____

_____

_____

Number
Answer

Cold Challenge: If I have 64 yogurt-covered raisins left over after our snowmen are completed, do we have enough for everyone in our class to each get two raisins? Why or why not?

Bite-Size Cracker Count

31

Food: any variety of bite-size cracker snacks

We have a large bag of bite-size cracker snacks for everyone in our class to enjoy. Let's count the crackers. If each of us receives 10 crackers, will we have enough crackers to go around? In the space below, draw a picture to show how you would solve this problem.

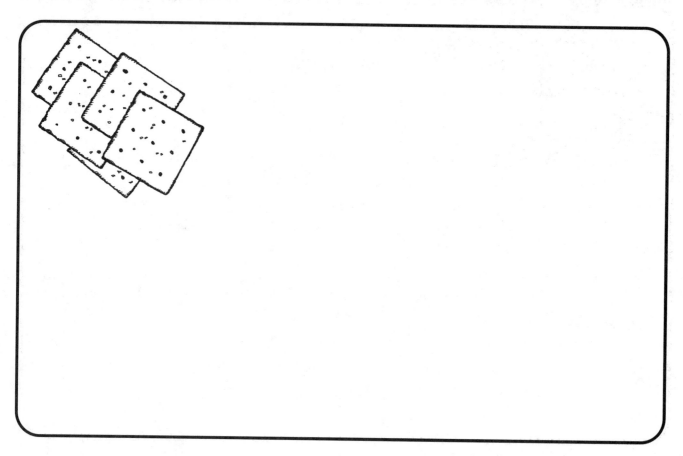

Solution Sentences: _____

_____

_____

Number
Answer

Cracker Challenge: If you bought a jumbo bag of crackers containing 600 crackers and you wanted to share them with 24 other people, what is the largest number of crackers each person can have?

Cool Carrots

Food: carrot sticks

Each carrot can make six carrot sticks. We have 11 carrots from which to cut the carrot sticks. How many carrot sticks will we have? Draw a picture to show what this would look like.

Solution Sentences: _____

_____

_____

Number
Answer [   ]

Carrot Challenge: With all of those carrot sticks, how many sticks will each person get? How could we share the leftover carrot sticks equally with our classmates?

Energy Booster Bars

Food: any nutritional energy bar

Read the nutrition information label on your bar to find the number of grams of protein. Draw a picture to show how many total grams of protein are in the bars we are using in our class.

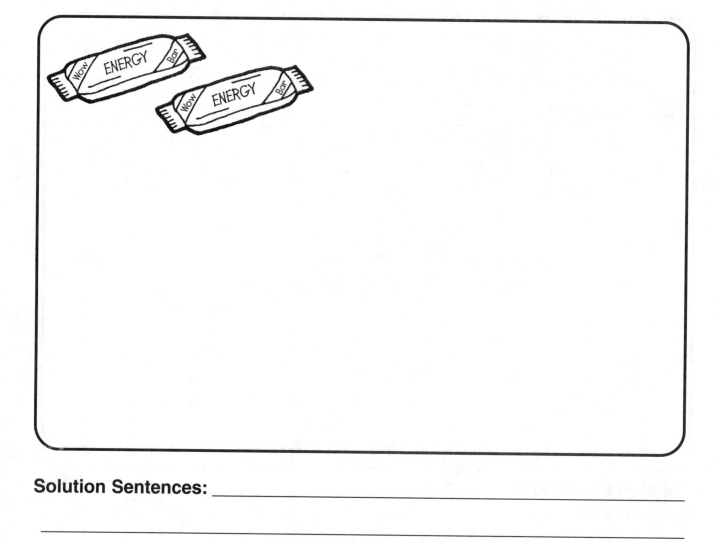

Solution Sentences: _____

_____

_____

Number
Answer

Calorie Challenge: If there are 130 calories in each bar, how many calories would be in three bars?

34

Pea Pod Problems

Food: peas in pods

From my garden, I picked 20 pea pods. In each pea pod there are three peas. How many peas are in my pods? In the space below, show what this would look like.

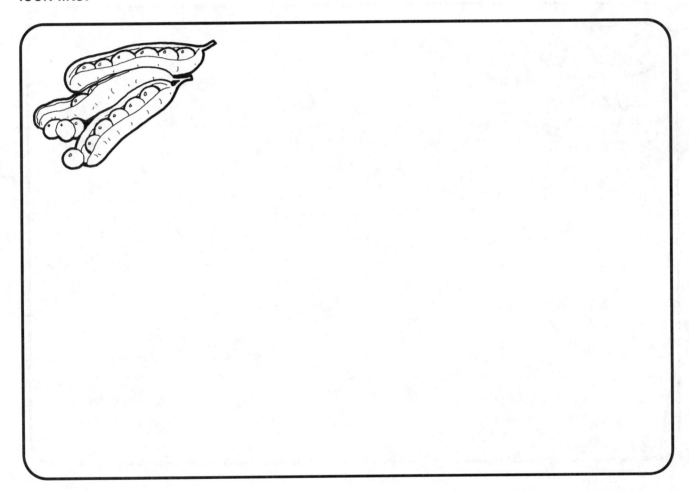

Solution Sentences: _____

_____

_____

Number
Answer

Pea Challenge: It takes me 15 seconds to get the peas out of each pea pod. How long will it take me to get all the peas out of the 20 pods I picked?

Gumdrop Groups

Food: gumdrops

You have been given 24 gumdrops. How many ways can you group them so that you use all of the gumdrops? Draw a picture to show your groups.

Solution Sentences: _____

_____

_____

Number
Answer
☐

Gumdrop Challenge: If each member of the class gave up three of his or her gumdrops to share with another class, how many gumdrops would they have to share?

Spooky Spiders

Food: round crackers, pretzel sticks, peanut butter, raisins

Teacher Note: Spooky Spiders can be made by placing peanut butter on a round cracker and arranging the halves of four pretzel sticks to represent legs. Add raisins for eyes.

If each cracker spider needs four pretzel sticks and one cracker, how many pretzels do we need and how many crackers do we need for our class to make spiders? (Count only the students who are here today.) Draw pictures to show what you would need.

Solution Sentences: _____

_____

_____

Number
Answer [ ]

Spider Challenge: If each roll of crackers has 24 crackers, how many crackers would three rolls of crackers contain?

Gingerbread People

37

Food: gingerbread cookies

If each person received one cookie and each cookie could have only three buttons, how many buttons do our 18 gingerbread cookies need? Draw a picture to show the number of buttons needed.

Solution Sentences: _____

_____

_____

Number Answer [   ]

Cookie Challenge: If each cookie has two eyes, how many eyes would 20 cookies have? How many eyes would 40 cookies have? How many eyes would eight cookies have? Do you see a number pattern in your answers? On the back of this paper, explain your thinking.

Eggs in a Basket

Food: yogurt-covered peanuts

Today we will count eggs in a basket. The "eggs" are yogurt-covered peanuts and the "basket" is a paper cup. If each student is given five eggs to place in his or her basket, how many eggs do we need for the class? Draw a picture to show how to solve this problem.

Solution Sentences: _____

_____

_____

Number
Answer [ ]

Egg Challenge: If our eggs (yogurt-covered peanuts) came in a bag of 200 eggs, how many eggs are left in the bag after we fill our baskets?

Ravishing Rings

39

Food: three-holed pretzels

Each pretzel has three rings or holes. If you **have seven pretzels, how many** holes do you have all together? **Show this in a drawing.**

Solution Sentences: _____

_____

_____

Number
Answer

Ring Challenge: If each person has 21 holes or rings, how many does our class have as a whole group? (Think about easy numbers to count.)

Rockin' Raisins

Food: raisins (small, individual boxes)

Today there are boxes of raisins for everyone in the class. If the boxes came in a package of two rows with six boxes in each row, how many packages were needed to supply each student with a box of raisins? Draw a picture to help you solve this problem.

Solution Sentences: _____

_____

_____

Number
Answer ☐

Raisin Challenge: You have one extra box of raisins. You must share it with two other people. How many raisins will each of you receive? Are there any left over? Show the solution to this problem in a number sentence or by drawing a picture.

Breaking Up the Bagels

Food: bagels

We have 36 bagels for our snack. There are three different kinds. How many of each kind of bagel do we have? Draw a picture to show how you would solve this problem.

Solution Sentences: _____

_____

_____

Number
Answer

Cream Cheese Challenge: If each tub of cream cheese can cover six bagels, how many tubs of cream cheese do we need to use on our 36 bagels?

Bountiful Brownies

42

Food: pan of brownies

We have a pan of brownies to share today. How many brownies will there be if we cut the brownies eight times down and six times across? Draw a picture to show this.

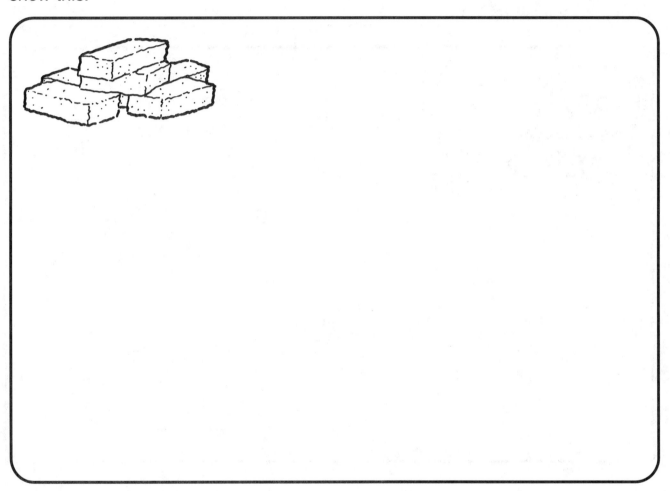

Solution Sentences: _____

_____

_____

Number
Answer [   ]

Cutting Challenge: How many brownies can each person in our class have from your cutting so that everyone gets an equal amount? How many leftovers are there?

Delicious Dried Fruit

43

Food: dried fruit

There are 42 pieces of dried fruit on the plate. We will share this snack with our class. How many pieces should each of us receive so that everyone has an equal amount? (There may be some left over.) Draw a picture to show how you would solve this problem.

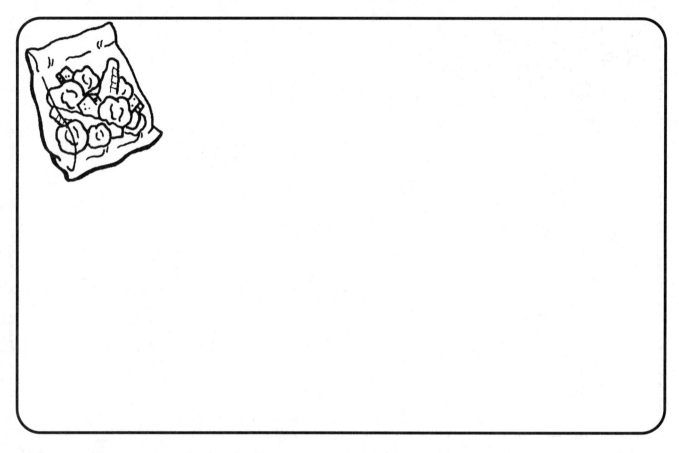

Solution Sentences: _____

_____

_____

Number
Answer [ ]

Dried Fruit Challenge: If you dry fruit yourself, it takes one and one-half days for each piece of fruit to dry. If you dried five pieces of fruit on separate days, how many days would it take to dry six pieces of fruit?

Sharing Sunflower Seeds

Food: sunflower seeds (out of the shell)

If there are 55 teaspoons of sunflower seeds in each bag, how many teaspoons can each person in our class have if we share the seeds equally? (There may be some left over.) Draw a picture to show how you would solve this problem.

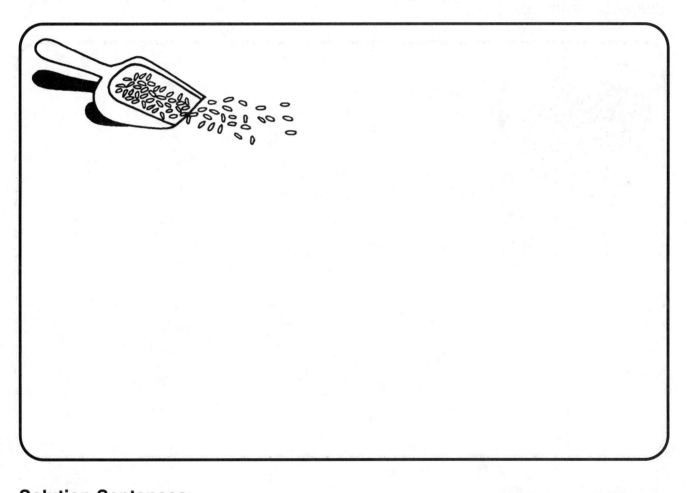

Solution Sentences: _____

_____

_____

Number
Answer ⬚

Sunny Challenge: Each sunflower produces 100 seeds. How many sunflowers were there if we have 800 seeds?

Pizza! Pizza!

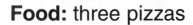

45

Food: three pizzas

It's pizza day! There is a total of 90 pieces of pepperoni on our pizzas. If we have three pizzas and they each have an equal number of pepperoni pieces, how many pepperoni pieces are on each pizza? In the space below show what this would look like.

Solution Sentences: _____

_____

_____

Number
Answer [   ]

Pizza Challenge: Each pizza has been cut into 12 slices. How many slices are there altogether? If we ate half of all the pizza we have, how many slices of pizza did we eat?

Cinco de Mayo Tortilla Chips

46

Food: tortillas

Each round tortilla can make four tortilla chips. You have 12 chips. How many round tortillas were used to make your chips? Draw a picture to show how you would solve this problem.

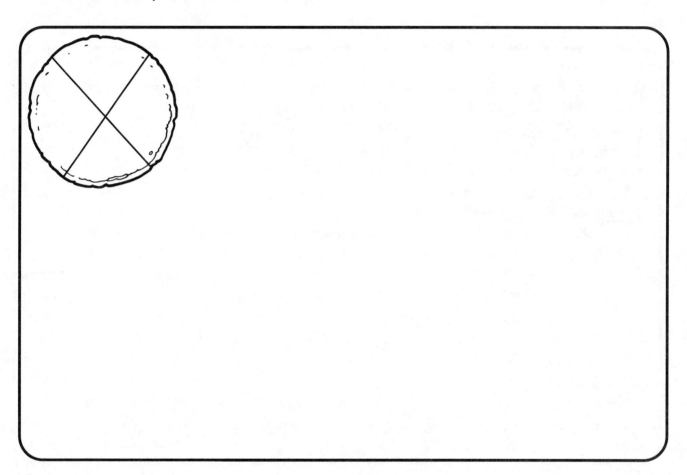

Solution Sentences: _____

_____

_____

Number
Answer

Tortilla Chip Challenge: How many tortillas would you need so that each person in the class receives two tortilla chips? (Each tortilla is divided into four chips.)

Mini Rice Cakes

Food: mini rice cakes

Rice cakes are a light and crunchy snack. If a serving size (the amount each of you will receive) is five rice cakes and there are 40 rice cakes in each bag, how many servings will there be in each bag? Draw a picture to help you solve this problem.

Solution Sentences: _____

_____

_____

Number
Answer

Rice Cake Challenge: How many bags do we need to supply each person in the class with a serving (five rice cakes each)? If each rice cake has 10 calories, how many calories are in half of the bag? How many calories are in the whole bag?

Powerful Popcorn

48

Food: bags of popcorn

Each bag of popcorn will serve six students. How many popcorn bags do we need for 18 students? Draw a picture to help you solve this problem.

Solution Sentences: _____

_____

_____

Number
Answer

Corny Challenge: If each bag takes five minutes to pop and there are three bags, what time will I finish popping the popcorn if I start at 10:30 a.m.? Show the time on a clock. Write the time in numbers if you can.

Quartered Quesadillas

49

Food: tortillas and cheese

It's tortilla time! First we have to decide how many tortillas we will need for the class if each of us is to receive ½ of a tortilla. Draw a picture to show this problem.

Solution Sentences: _____

_____

_____

Number
Answer

Quesadilla Challenge: Each quesadilla takes 30 seconds to cook. If each quesadilla is cooked separately, how many seconds long will it take for all of our quesadillas to be ready to eat? About how many minutes is this?

Bonkers for Bananas

50

Food: bananas

Each person in our class will receive ½ of a banana. Count the number of students in the class today. How many bananas are needed? Complete the chart on page 70 to help you solve the problem. Then draw a picture in the space below to show how you solved the problem.

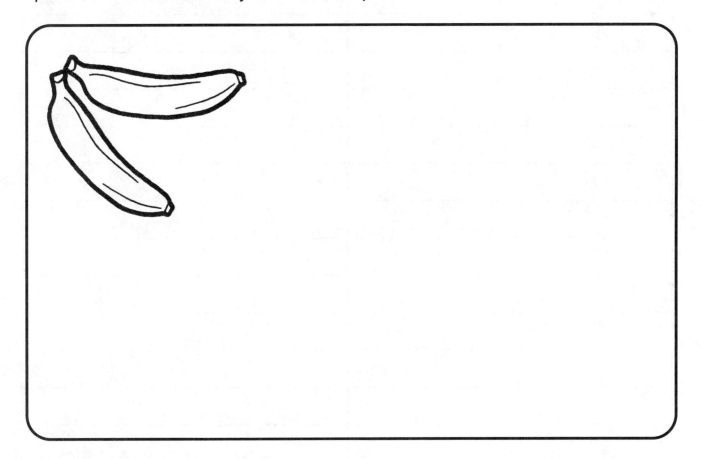

Solution Sentences: _____

_____

_____

Number
Answer

Banana Challenge: If every five bananas weigh one pound (.45 kg), how many pounds would 20 bananas weigh?

Bonkers for Bananas *(cont.)*

50

After you have completed this chart, use the information to solve the problem on page 69.

Number of People	Number of Bananas
2	1
4	2

Fruity Fractions

Food: fruit snacks (variety of colors or shapes)

We will use today's fruit snacks to help us understand fractions. You will each receive two handfuls of fruit snacks in a bag. Write a fraction to represent each kind of fruit you have in your bag. Draw a picture to show each fraction and then write that fraction.

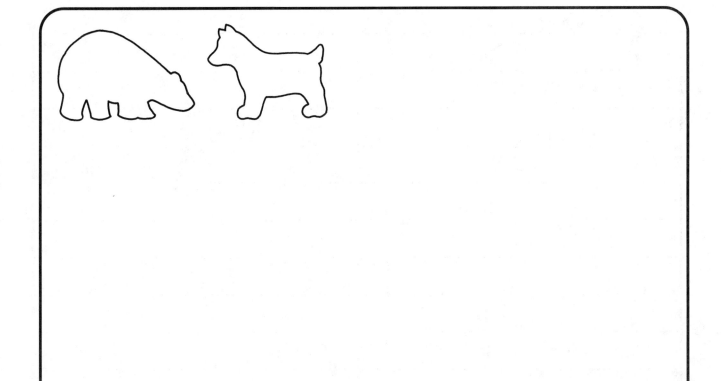

Solution Sentences: _____

_____

_____

Number
Answer ☐

Fruity Challenge: If each bag contains eight fruit snacks and there are 10 bags per box, what is the total number of fruit snacks in one box?

Awesome Apples

52

Food: apples

Today we will be enjoying apple slices. Get together with three other students.
In your group, you will share three apples equally. If each apple is sliced into
four equal parts, how many slices will each of you receive? What fraction is
this? Draw a picture to show how you would solve this problem.

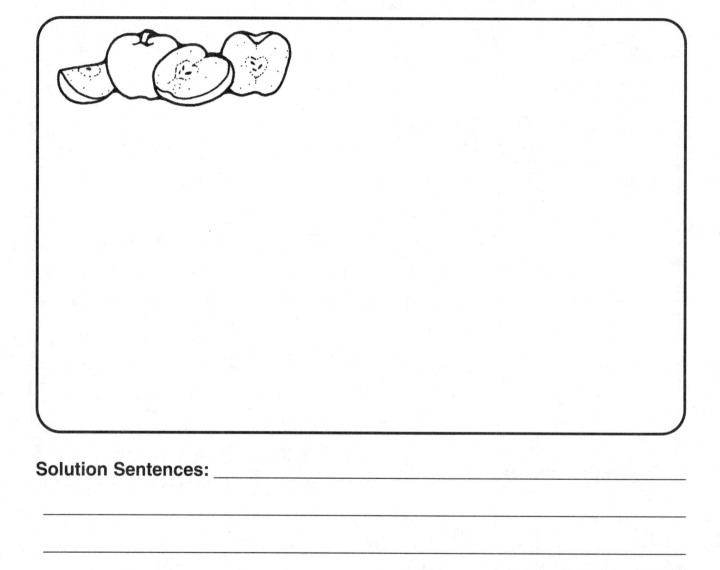

Solution Sentences: _____

_____

_____

Number
Answer [   ]

Apple Slice Challenge: If your apple slices were cut in half, what would each
apple slice represent as a fraction?

Pretzel Portions

Food: bags of pretzel sticks

Today we will use our pretzel snacks to help us learn more about fractions. Get together with three other people. Place three or four handfuls of pretzels on a paper towel and count them. If you have an odd number of pretzels, remove one from the pile. Now work together to divide the pretzels evenly among the four of you. What fraction of the pile did each of you receive? Draw a picture to show what you did to solve this problem.

Solution Sentences: _____

_____

Number Answer [   ]

Pretzel Challenge: What other fractions can you think of to show how many pretzels each of you received?

Colorful Candies

Food: any candy-coated treat (assorted colors)

For today's activity you will need two or three handfuls of our candy treat. Sort them by color. What fraction do you have of each color? (Remember, a fraction is a part of a whole.) Draw a picture to help you solve this problem.

Solution Sentences: Describe what you did to find the fractional number for each color.

_____

_____

_____

Candy Challenge: If a large bag costs $2.50, how much would four bags of candy cost?

Goofy Graham Crackers

Food: graham crackers

Use your graham cracker snack to solve this problem. If each person in our class gets one half a cracker, how many whole crackers do we need for our class? Draw a picture that shows how you solved the problem.

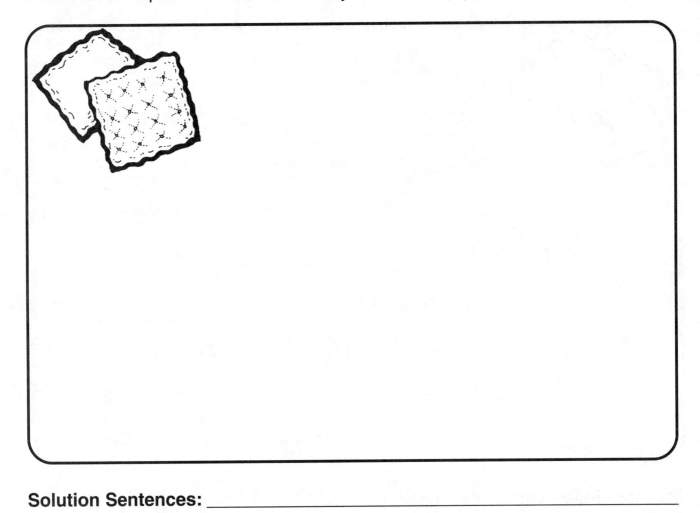

Solution Sentences: _____

_____

_____

Number
Answer [   ]

Cracker Challenge: If there are two packages of 20 crackers in a box and they can be broken in fourths, how many fourths are there?

Patriotic Painting

56

Food: graham crackers and frosting (red, white, blue)

Each person in our class is going to paint $\frac{1}{3}$ of his or her graham cracker red. What part of everyone's cracker will not be painted red? Draw a picture to show how you painted your crackers.

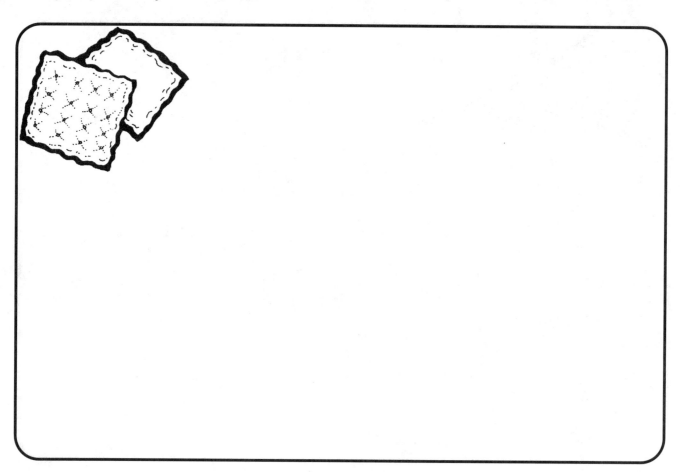

Solution Sentences: _____

_____

_____

Number
Answer

Cracker Challenge: If each person has three parts to the cracker, how many total parts are there in our class?

Jellybean Jumble

Food: jellybeans (assorted colors)

Today we will use our jelly bean snack to practice fractions. You will need 12 jellybeans. Sort the jellybeans by color and draw a picture of your results below. What fraction represents the color with the most jellybeans?

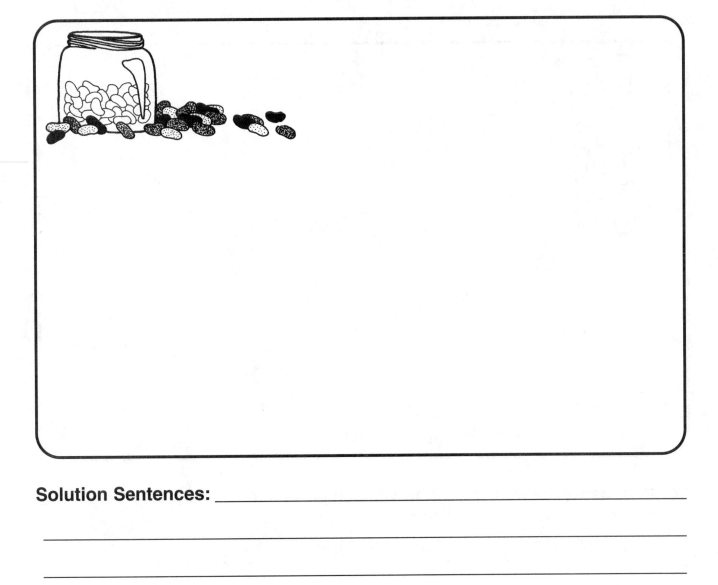

Solution Sentences: _____

_____

_____

Number
Answer

Jellybean Challenge: Write a fraction for each of the other jellybean colors. Can you add all the fractions together? The answer represents the whole group of jellybeans. What fraction is used to show this?

Biggest Breadstick

58

Food: different lengths of breadsticks for each group

Get together with two or three other students. Using your breadsticks with your group, measure each breadstick and record the length of each. Draw a picture of each breadstick and record its length next to it. Find the longest breadstick in your group.

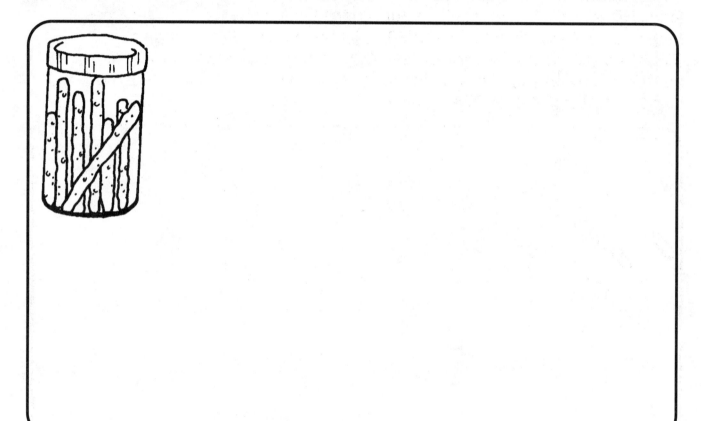

Solution Sentences: Describe how you can prove that you have found the longest breadstick.

_____

_____

Number
Answer

Breadstick Challenge: Add up all of the lengths of your breadsticks. What is the total length of your group's breadsticks?

Lengthy Licorice

Food: licorice sticks

Teacher Note: If classroom rulers are not available, you can use the inch ruler pattern provided in the last section of this book. Use index stock to reproduce as many copies as you need.

Your math snack today is a licorice stick. Use an inch ruler to measure the length of your licorice stick. Cut your licorice into one-inch (2.5 cm) pieces. Measure the items listed on page 80 by using one of the inch pieces. (Remember to throw the used piece away when you finish this problem. You can eat the other pieces.) Draw a picture to show how you measured each of the items. How long is the longest item?

Solution Sentences: _____

_____

_____

Number
Answer

Licorice Challenge: If everyone in our class discards the one-inch (2.5 cm) piece he or she used for measuring, how many inches were discarded in all?

Lengthy Licorice *(cont.)*

59

Use your one inch (2.5 cm) piece of licorice to measure the following items:

1. a pencil   _____

2. length of your desk   _____

3. your pointing finger   _____

4. your arm from wrist to elbow   _____

5. a new crayon   _____

6. the width of a piece of notebook paper   _____

7. the length of your shoe   _____

Pretzel Log Run

Food: 12 pretzel logs (Pretzel sticks may be substituted.)

Place your pretzel logs end to end. Use a centimeter ruler to measure the length of all the logs in a row. How many centimeters long would two sets of 12 logs placed end to end equal? Show what this would look like.

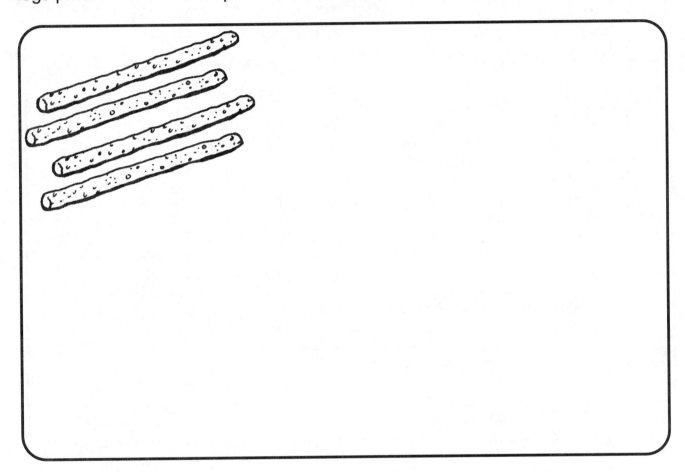

Solution Sentences: _____

_____

_____

Number
Answer

Pretzel Challenge: Use all of the 12 logs to make the sides of a square. Measure around the shape. This is called finding the perimeter. What is the perimeter of your square? How does it compare to the length of the logs placed end to end?

Cheese Cut-Ups

Food: sliced cheese

Each of you has a slice of cheese for your math snack. Use a plastic knife to slice your cheese into several strips, each about the same size. Use a centimeter ruler to measure the length of one strip of cheese. What would be the total length (about how many centimeters) of the cheese strips placed end to end? Draw a picture to show how you arrived at this number.

Solution Sentences: _____

_____

_____

Number Answer	

Cheese Challenge: If each member of the class cuts a cheese strip and all the strips are placed end to end, how many centimeters (cm) in length will the one long strip equal? Explain how you solved the problem.

Cracker Creation

Food: 10 crackers of various shapes and sizes

Today we have cracker shapes for our math snack. You each have 10 crackers. Use all of your crackers to create an object. The crackers must all touch so that the parts of your creation are connected. Draw your new creation in the space below. How many of each shape did you use to make your creation?

Solution Sentences: _____

_____

_____

Number
Answer

Cracker Challenge: Can you change the positions of only five crackers to make a different object? Remember, the parts of your creation must be connected.

Pineapple Circles

Food: pineapple chunks

Today we have fresh pineapples to share. Each of you will receive pineapple chunks. Arrange the chunks to form a circle (pineapple ring) and count how many chunks you used. If each student uses the same number of chunks to make his or her circle, how many chunks would be needed for all the pineapple rings in the class? Draw a picture to show your solution to this problem.

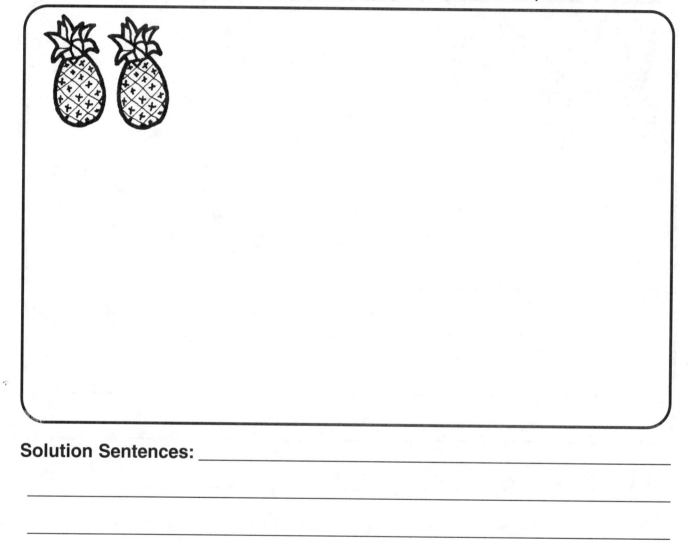

Solution Sentences: _____

_____

_____

Number
Answer

Chunky Challenge: If one pineapple can make 10 pineapple circles, how many pineapple circles could we make from eight pineapples? If each circle is made from 10 pineapple chunks, how many chunks would be needed?

A Tasty Tessellation

Food: any triangle-shaped cracker

Today we have triangle-shaped crackers for math snack. Create a tessellation by arranging 15 crackers on a paper towel. Do your best to show that image in the space below. You may want to add details or designs to your tessellation to make it special.

Solution Sentences: What makes your creation a tessellation?

_____

_____

What would not make it a tessellation?

_____

_____

Cracker Challenge: If you used 15 triangles, how many sides do you have in all? Explain your answer.

Granola Geometry

65

Food: granola bars

Each of you has been given a granola bar. Place the bar on a clean surface and measure it. Measure the length and width of your bar. Next measure to find out how high your bar stands off the surface. Now multiply the length times the width. Multiply this total times the height. This number represents the volume of your bar. Draw a picture of your granola bar. Try to make it three-dimensional. Label it with the numbers from above. What is the volume of your granola bar?

Solution Sentences: _____

_____

Number
Answer

Granola Challenge: Using the volume of your granola bar, find the total volume of all the bars in your class.

Star Cookie Geometry

Food: star-shaped cookies

Each of you has been given three star cookies. Each cookie star has five triangle shapes in it. Draw a picture to show how each triangle would look. How many triangles would seven stars have?

Solution Sentences: _____

_____

_____

Number
Answer [ ]

Star Challenge: When you take the triangles off each star, what shape is left? If you have seven pentagons, how many sides in all do you have for those seven shapes?

Cracker Squares

Food: square-shaped crackers

We have tasty crackers for our math snack. If you have been given 12 crackers and all of them are squares, how many corners do you have in all? Draw a picture to show how you solved this problem.

Solution Sentences: _____

_____

_____

Number
Answer [   ]

Crisper Challenge: If your crackers are four centimeters wide, how long would your 12 crackers be if you lined them up side by side?

Sizing Up Squares

Food: square-shaped crackers

For today's snack, each of you has 12 square crackers. Use all the crackers to make a larger square. If each square cracker represents a square unit (the length and width are the same), how many square units are in the larger square? Draw a picture to show what this looks like.

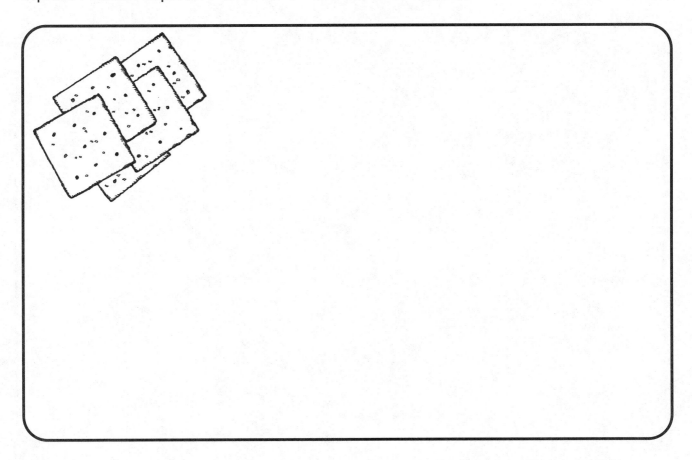

Solution Sentences: _____

_____

_____

                                                         Number ⬚
                                                         Answer

Square Challenge: Use all 12 crackers to make a rectangle that is not a square. Can you make other rectangles? How many square units are in each rectangle?

Awesome Oranges

Food: slices and one orange

We will have oranges for our math snack today. The shape of an orange is called a *sphere*. We can cut our orange sphere into slices. If every eight orange slices makes one sphere, how many spheres will 48 orange slices make? Draw a picture to help you solve this problem.

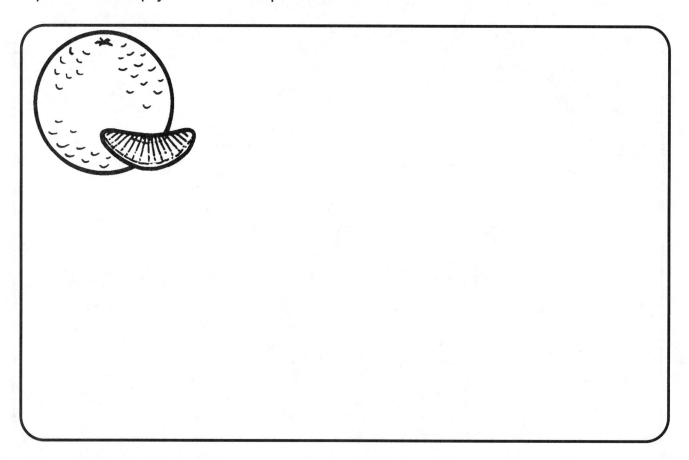

Solution Sentences: _____

_____

_____

Number
Answer [   ]

Sphere Challenge: Each orange slice has four seeds. How many seeds would be in our 48 slices? How many slices would there be if there were only 24 seeds?

Luscious Lollipops

10

Food: lollipops (sugarless, if possible)

Each box of lollipops costs $3.50. If there are 50 lollipops in each box, how much does each lollipop cost? Draw a picture to show how you would solve this problem.

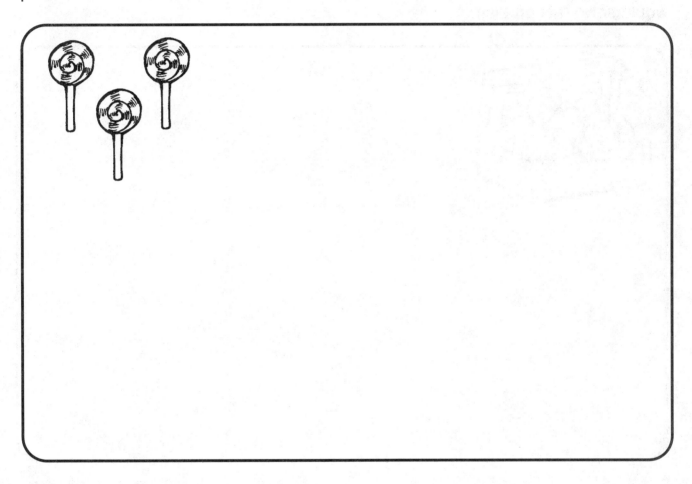

Solution Sentences: _____

_____

_____

Number
Answer

Costly Challenge: If you want to buy 100 of these lollipops for a party, will a 10 dollar bill be enough to pay the cashier? Explain your answer.

Dime-a-Donut Holes

Food: donut holes

For today's snack we have delicious donut holes. In the box, there were 48 (four dozen) donut holes. If each donut hole cost 10 cents, how much did all 48 donut holes cost? In the space below, draw the donut holes to show how you would solve this problem.

Solution Sentences: _____

_____

_____

Number
Answer [   ]

Cheap Challenge: If I gave the clerk a five-dollar bill, how much change should I get back from buying the donut holes above? If I had a 10-dollar bill, could I buy two boxes of donut holes? Explain your answers.

Cereal Cents

72

Food: breakfast cereal

Today we have some crunchy cereal for our math snack. If each box of cereal costs $2.40 and there are 12 servings in a box, what is the cost of one serving? Draw a picture to help you solve this problem.

Solution Sentences: _____

_____

_____

Number
Answer   ☐

Cereal Challenge: What is the total cost of all the servings in our class? How many boxes of cereal are needed so that each student can have a serving?

Pricing Pizza

Food: pizzas (enough for one slice per student)

We have pizza slices for today's math snack. If each large pizza costs $12.00 and is cut into 12 slices, how much does each slice cost? Draw a picture to show your solution to this problem.

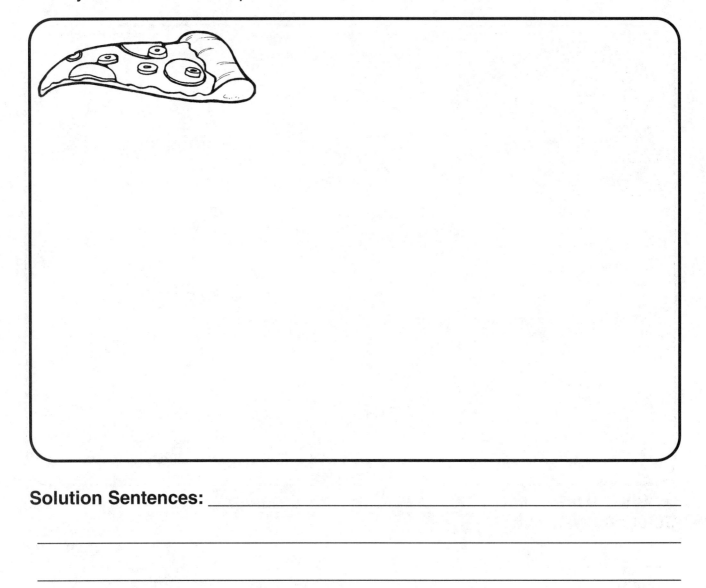

Solution Sentences: _____

_____

_____

Number
Answer
[   ]

Pizza Challenge: If a single slice of pizza at the pizzeria costs $1.50, how much money do you save with a slice of pizza from a whole pie? How much money do you save altogether on individual slices when you buy a whole pizza?

Fortune Cookie Math

74

Food: children's fortune cookies

We have fortune cookies for our math snack today. If each fortune cookie costs $.07, how much will 30 fortune cookies cost? In the space below, show how you would solve this problem.

Solution Sentences: _____

_____

_____

Number
Answer

Cookie Challenge: If the fortune cookies were on sale for $.05 per cookie and each class member was given two cookies, how much would our class save?

Candy Calculation

Food: individually wrapped hard candies (sugarless, if possible)

If each bag of today's candy treats costs $2.00 and there are 40 candies in the bag, how much does each candy cost? Draw a picture to show your solution to this problem.

Solution Sentences: _____

_____

_____

Number
Answer

Candy Challenge: If each student receives two candies, how many bags would be needed for the class? What would the cost be for the bags? Explain your answers.

Time for Toast

Food: bread for toasting

We will make toast for our math snack today. We can toast two pieces of bread at a time. Each piece of bread takes 20 seconds to toast. How long will it take to toast 22 pieces of bread? Draw a picture to show how you solved this problem.

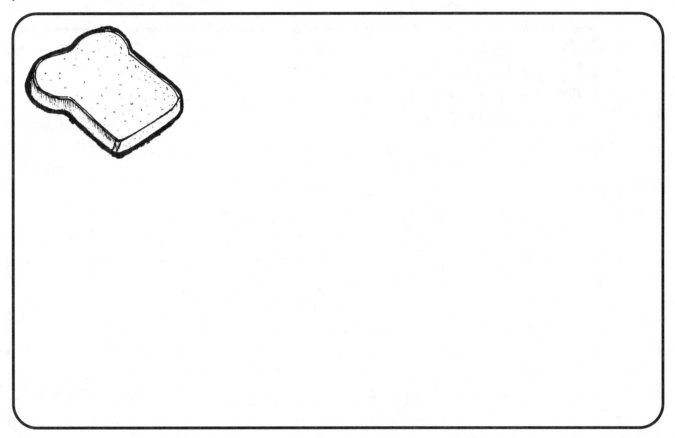

Solution Sentences: _____

_____

_____

Number
Answer

Cinnamon Challenge: You want to add cinnamon and sugar to your toast. The cinnamon costs $3.45, and the sugar costs $2.35. Can you buy these ingredients if you have $5.00? If you can, how much money would you have left? If you cannot, how much more money would you need to be able to get the extras?

Clocking the Cookies

11

Food: chocolate chip cookies

We have homemade chocolate chip cookies today. There are four dozen chocolate chip cookies. Each dozen took the same amount of time to bake. If it took one hour to make all 48 cookies, how long did each dozen cookies take to bake? In the box, show how you would solve this problem.

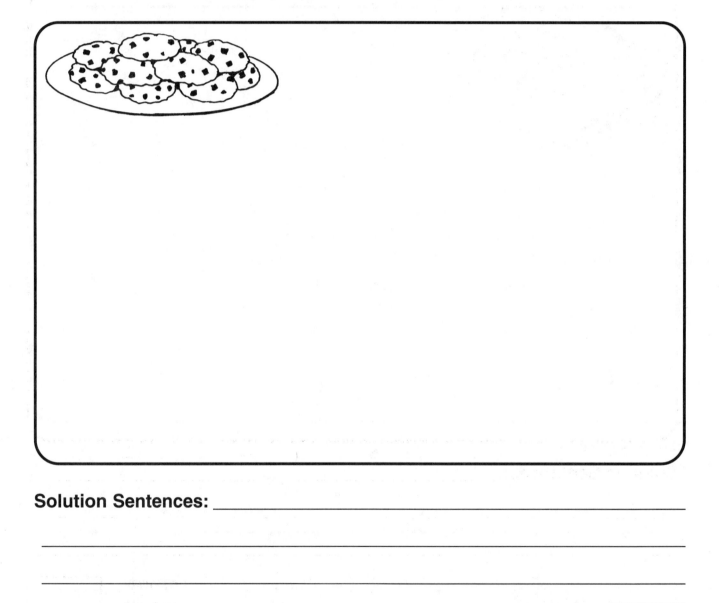

Solution Sentences: _____

_____

_____

Number
Answer ☐

Chocolate Chip Challenge: If each cookie has seven chocolate chips in it, how many chocolate chips are in our four dozen cookies?

Wacky Wafers

78

Food: vanilla wafers

When the wafers were baked, each dozen cookies took 12 minutes to bake in the oven. How long in all did it take for 36 wafers to bake? Draw a picture to show how you solved this problem.

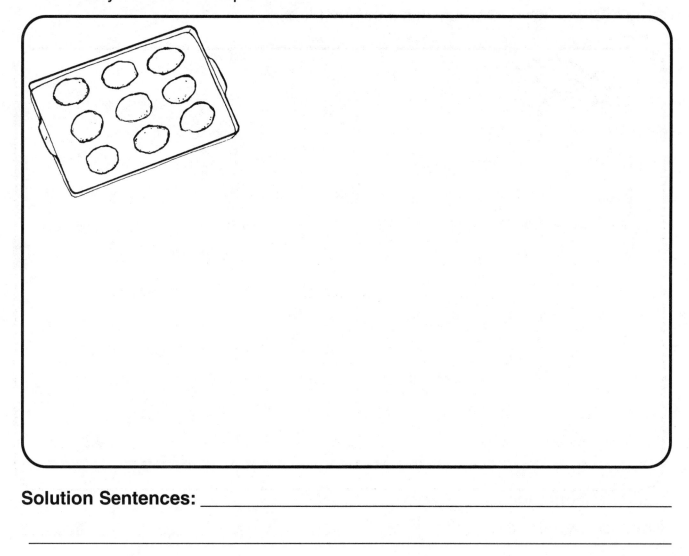

Solution Sentences: _____

_____

_____

Number
Answer ☐

Cookie Challenge: In 48 minutes, how many dozen wafers could you bake? In one hour, how many dozen wafers could you bake?

79

Apple Chewing Time

Food: any variety of apples

Our math snack today is an apple. You will need a clock with a second hand. Time how many seconds it takes to thoroughly chew a bite of the apple. If you take 10 more bites to finish the apple, how many seconds of chewing have you done? Show how you would solve this problem.

Solution Sentences: _____

_____

_____

Number
Answer

Chewy Challenge: If every student in the classroom takes the same number of bites and the same time to chew each bite of apple, how many total minutes does the entire class take to finish their apples?

Crackers and Cheese Time

Food: any variety of snack crackers, slices of cheese

You will need a clock with a second hand, a plastic knife, and a partner. Have your partner time (in seconds) how long it takes for you to cut five small pieces of cheese and place each of them on top of a cracker. At this same rate, how long will it take you to top 35 crackers with cheese? In the space below, draw your solution to this problem.

Solution Sentences: _____

_____

_____

Number
Answer [ ]

Cracker Challenge: If it takes 30 seconds to top 10 crackers with cheese, how many crackers can be topped in 3 minutes if the rate stays the same? Explain how you solved this problem.

Creating Graphs

As an extension to the regular math snacks program, graphing a type of food or food preference can be effective. One effective method of graphing is to write a question on the board or on a poster. The question should be written exactly as it appears on the student's paper. Ask the students to create graphs using a variety of methods, depending upon what is most efficient in your classroom. For example, if you have a white board, you may write the question and have each student use a dry-erase marker to graph the information that provides the answer. If you use a chalkboard, you may write the question and provide students with sticky notes to use as data markers. They can then write their names on their sticky notes, come up to the board, and place their votes on the class graph.

Another effective method of creating a graph is to write the graph question on poster board or chart paper and have each student contribute to the graph by gluing on a piece of cut paper, coloring in the information on the graph, or using a sticky note to indicate a preference. An overhead projector can also be used as a means of creating a graph and presenting results. Students can actually contribute their data on an overhead transparency and share it with the class.

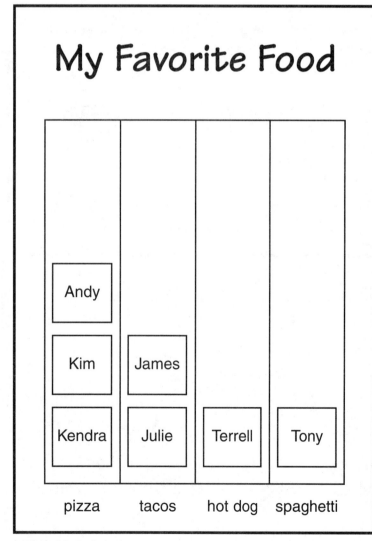

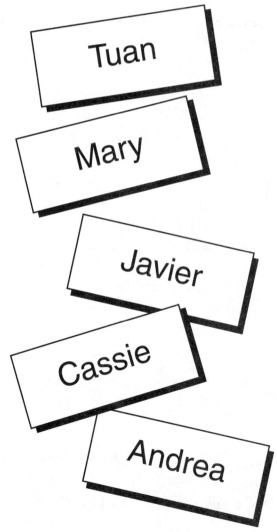

Creating Graphs *(cont.)*

After data has been collected, students should transfer the information to their individual papers. Once this is done, they need to communicate as much about the data as they can. It is most beneficial to do several class graphs without paperwork prior to having the students use their pencils. By doing this, students begin to develop vocabulary that can later be used to express their observations about the class graphs. While discussing the results of the graph, use words like *most, least, similar, total, difference,* and *conclusion*. This vocabulary becomes a natural part of their answers when they get used to hearing it.

You may want to delay providing the snack until immediately after the graph is finished. Presenting the most popular snack according to the graph is one more way to show students the value of real-life information and how their decisions and votes do have an impact.

The way the information is represented is not as important as the interpretation of the graph data. A blank grid is provided on page 131. This may be used by students to create graphs based on the results of a class graphing activity. The grid can also be used to represent the students' results from their own graphing activities and data collection.

Several different types of graphing activities are presented on the following student pages. For some of the activities, students are asked to use class data to complete their activity pages. A few of the activities require that students use a snack to gather their own information and then graph the results.

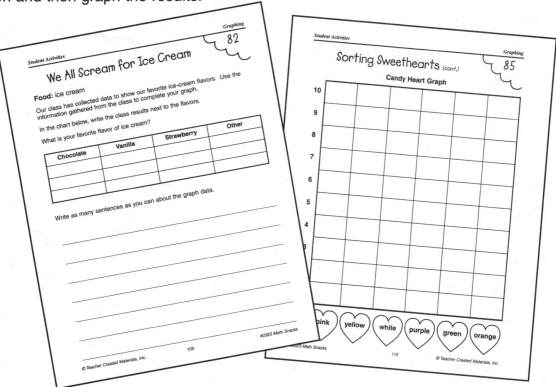

The key to all the graphing activities is to make them important to the students. When students realize that graphing is another safe environment in which to communicate about math, their interest peaks.

Jumping Jellybeans

Food: jellybeans

Our class has collected data to show our favorite jelly bean colors. Use the information to complete your graph.

In the chart below, write the class results next to the colors.

What is your favorite jellybean color?

red		purple	
orange		pink	
yellow		white	
green		black	

Now use the correct colors to graph your data on a graph grid.

Write as many sentences about the graph data as you can.

_____

_____

_____

_____

_____

On the back of this paper arrange the colors from least favorite to most favorite colors.

82

We All Scream for Ice Cream

Food: ice cream

Our class has collected data to show our favorite ice-cream flavors. Use the information gathered from the class to complete your graph.

In the chart below, write the class results next to the flavors.

What is your favorite flavor of ice cream?

Chocolate	Vanilla	Strawberry	Other

Write as many sentences as you can about the graph data.

_____

_____

_____

_____

_____

_____

After Lunch Crunch Pictograph

Food: peanuts, almonds, raisins, cashews, candy-coated
chocolates (a handful of this mixture)

Sort your goodies. Draw a picture to show how many of each item you have.
Draw one picture for each one of the items. For example, if you have five
almonds, draw five pictures next to the word almonds.

candy-coated chocolates
almonds
peanuts
raisins
cashews

Crunchy Challenge: Using graph paper, make a bar graph to show how many
of each item you have. Remember to label your graph, write about the most and
least, and note any ties among the items.

Candy Sort Pie Graph

84

Food: any assorted candies with at least five different colors
(You will need only five of these. Put aside additional colors.)

Gather 10 candies and sort them by color. Count how many you have of each color. Fill in the pie graph on page 108 to show how many there are of each color. For example, if you have two red candies, color two parts of the pie (circle) red.

Write as many sentences as you can about your sorted candy and how you completed your pie graph.

_____

_____

_____

_____

_____

_____

_____

_____

_____

Candy Sort Pie Graph *(cont.)*

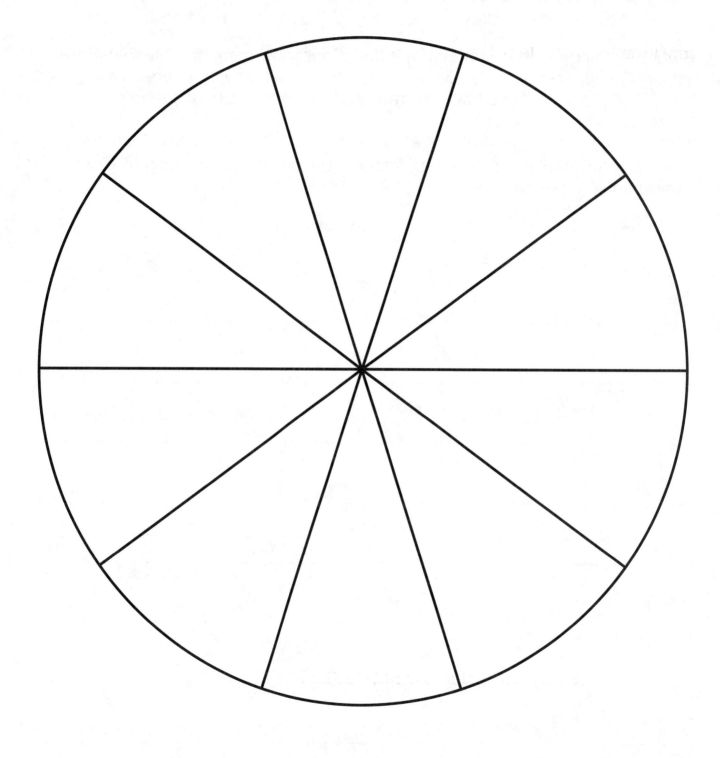

Graph Title

Class Cereal Selection

86

Food: six different breakfast cereals

Our class has collected data to show our favorite breakfast cereals. You will use the information gathered from the class to complete your own graph.

In the chart below, write the class results next to the cereal favorites. Use the information to complete your graph.

What is your favorite type of cereal?

Cereal Name	How Many Students Chose This Cereal?

Write as many sentences about the graph data as you can.

_____

_____

_____

_____

_____

Cereal Challenge: On the back of this paper, plan a healthful breakfast using something from each one of the food groups.

Fabulous Fruit Graph

Food: apples, bananas, oranges, grapes, pears, other fruits

Use the information collected from the class to complete your graph. In the chart below use tally marks (⃧⃧⃧⃧⃧) to show what each student chose as his or her favorite fruit. Use one tally for each student. Make a bar graph to show the results.

What is your favorite kind of fruit?

apples	
bananas	
oranges	
grapes	
pears	
other	

Write as many sentences about the graph data as you can.

_____

_____

_____

_____

_____

Fruity Challenge: Choose one of the fruits from the graph above and create a math story problem. Remember to use math words and to ask a question you can solve.

Using Estimation for Math Snacks

Estimation is an important math strategy. Working with estimation can be an enjoyable addition to the daily math snacks activities. Children love to guess how many there are of something and then count to see how close they came to the actual number answer. One way to provide students with practice in estimating is to present them with a small sampling of a snack and have them estimate and count the items they have in front of them. Another method is to provide one large class snack and take several guesses as to how many there are of the item before counting the entire snack in front of the class. As you do this you are providing students with models of how to group and of the various strategies used for counting.

You can also take guesses on a large class snack and divide the counting responsibility among small groups of students. When each group has finished counting its sample, you can model for the class, showing how you add two-digit and three-digit numbers to find a total.

Another estimation strategy is to use the serving information on snack packages to model how you, as the teacher, often decide whether a snack will be enough for the class. It is also a way to show the multiplication of larger numbers in a real-life setting.

Yet another estimation strategy requires that you reveal more and more information until the students can accurately determine the total number of items in the container. This method takes a little more preparation on the teacher's part. Have students guess a total number based only on the external size of the container. After the students have recorded their initial guesses, remind them that they cannot change the initial answer, but they can alter the following answers once you tell them more information. Next, tell the students how many of the item fit inside one cup. At this point, they can write a new answer down, or they can record the old answer if they feel it is still a reasonable answer. Finally, tell the students how many cups fill the container. Now, the students do the majority of their thinking as they know how many cups of items are in the container and how many items are in each cup. Require that they show their thinking processes on paper and come up with final estimations as to how many items are in the container. As with all math snacks activities, students should communicate their answers and their thinking. When all estimation attempts have been made, count the items to find the actual total.

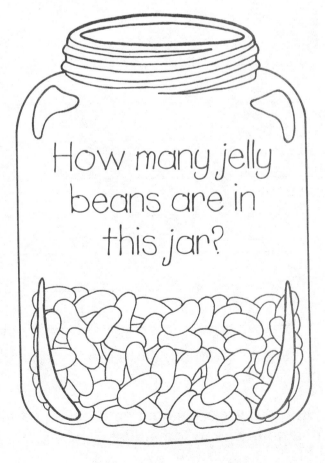

How many jelly beans are in this jar?

Easy Estimating

Food: any small snack

Use the snack provided to complete the following information.

The item I am estimating is _____.

My first estimate is _____.

I know that there are _____ items in each cup.

My second estimate is _____.

I know there are _____ cups of items in the container.

My third estimate is _____.

Explain or show why you think your third estimate is correct.

_____

_____

_____

_____

_____

_____

_____

_____

My teacher told me there are approximately _____ items in the container.

On the back of this paper, draw a picture to show how close your original estimate was to the actual number.

89

Boxed Raisins Estimation

Food: small boxes of raisins (one box per student)

Use the snack provided to complete the following information.

1. Without opening your box of raisins, estimate how many raisins there are in your box.

My Estimate [   ]

2. Open your box and count the top layer. How many raisins do you think are in your box now? You can keep your same answer if you still think it is correct.

My Estimate [   ]

3. Now empty your raisin box and count how many raisins you have. How many raisins do you have in all?

_____

_____

_____

How did you count your raisins to arrive at this number?

_____

_____

_____

4. How close was your estimation to the actual raisin count?

_____

_____

Raisin Challenge: If each box of raisins costs $.25, how much does a package of six boxes cost? How much did all three packages cost in all?

90

Cereal Count

Food: any breakfast cereal with bite-sized pieces

Use the snack provided to complete the following information.

1. Estimate how many cereal pieces will fill a drinking cup.

   My Estimate [＿＿＿＿＿]

2. Count how many cereal pieces actually fill the cup.

   Actual Number [＿＿＿＿＿]

3. Using your original estimate, how many pieces do you think would be in $\frac{1}{8}$ of a cup (30 mL)?

Solution Sentences: _____

_____

_____

_____

_____

_____

_____

_____

Number
Answer [＿＿＿＿＿]

Cereal Challenge: If there are 10 cups of cereal in a box, about how many cereal pieces are in one box? (Use the information from above.)

Marshmallow Measuring

Food: miniature marshmallows

Use the snack provided to complete the following information.

1. How many marshmallows do you think will fit in a paper drinking cup?

   My Estimate [   ]

2. Fill your cup and count how many marshmallows fit.

   How many marshmallows are in your cup? _____

3. If there are 10 cups of marshmallows and each cup has 15 marshmallows, how many marshmallows are there in all?

Solution Sentences: _____

_____

_____

_____

_____

_____

_____

_____

Number
Answer [   ]

Marshmallow Challenge: Each cup of marshmallows weighs approximately 1.25 ounces (35 g). How much would 10 cups of marshmallows weigh?

End-to-End Estimation

Food: packaged sticks of gum (17–20 piece package)

Use the snack provided to complete the following information.

1. Estimate the length of all the sticks of gum in the package, placed end to end.

   My Estimate [   ]

2. Write your ideas about how you might be able to bring your estimate closer to the actual length.

   _____

   _____

   _____

   _____

   _____

   _____

   _____

   _____

3. Find the actual measurement of the line of sticks of gum placed end to end.

   Actual Measurement [   ]

How close were you to the actual length of the line?

   _____

Gummy Challenge: Imagine that you attached your sticks of gum to form a 12-foot (3.6m) gum roll. Estimate the number of sticks you would need if the sticks were place end to end.

93

Shoebox Brownies

Food: brownies cut into two-inch (5 cm) squares (enough for one per student)

For this activity, you and your classmates will use the class snack and a shoebox. (Line the shoebox with paper towels or waxed paper.)

1. If our brownies are cut into two-inch (5 cm) squares, is there enough room in the shoebox to place one brownie for each student?

   _____

2. Do you think there will be room left over, or will we need another box?

   _____

3. What is your estimate?

   _____

4. Write your ideas about how you arrived at this estimate.

   _____

   _____

   _____

   _____

5. Your teacher will place the brownies in the shoebox. Explain how your estimate compares to the actual number of brownies that fit in the shoebox.

   _____

   _____

   _____

   _____

Extensions, Tools, and Incentives

120

Computer Activity

Extensions

Cookie Taste Test

For this activity you will need access to a computer paint program, five kinds of cookies broken into bite-sized pieces, and five differently colored paper plates. Students will collect, organize, and graph data and then display it on the computer. Use the following lesson plan or adapt it to meet your classroom needs.

Note: Students should be familiar with the paint and draw tools in a computer paint program.

Before Using the Computer

- Create the graph template on page 122 and save it in a file.
- Break the cookies into bite-sized pieces and place them on differently colored plates. Each type of cookie should be on a different plate.
- Have students taste the different brands of cookies and decide which brand they like best. They should remember which color plate the cookie was on.

At the Computer

- Lead a class discussion on the cookie preferences by asking students to raise their hands for the plate of cookies they liked best. Count the number of raised hands for each color and record these numbers on a chart.
- Display the graph template in the paint program on the monitor. Explain to students that they are going to use a circle for each person who voted for a particular brand of cookie.
- Ask students how many of them liked the cookies on a particular plate color. Have a student draw the number of circles in the matching colored box that represents the number of children who preferred the cookies on that plate.
- Ask about the remaining plates and student preferences. For each, have students fill in the graph with the appropriate number of circles.
- Lead a discussion about the graph by asking questions similar to the following: Which cookie was preferred by most of the students? Which cookie was liked the least? How many students liked the second favorite cookie? Is there a kind of cookie that no one liked? Can you think of any other ways to show the same information about the cookies?
- Tell students that they will have the opportunity to create their own picture graph by selecting the symbol they want to use to represent the number of children who liked a particular cookie.
- Have students print their graphs and close the file without saving it. This will allow others to use the blank graph.

Additional Activities

- Different types of food can be used instead of cookies.
- Students can create graphs of different types, such as a line graph or pie chart, using the original data on the cookies.
- Students can create problem questions based on the graph for others to answer.

Computer Activity *(cont.)*

Cookie Taste Test Graph

_____ plate color	
_____ plate color	
_____ plate color	
_____ plate color	
_____ plate color	

 **= a vote for that type of cookie**

Food and Nutrition Activity

Teacher Note: Remind students that while snacks are a welcomed treat, they should keep daily snacks to a minimum and try to choose those that provide the most nutritional value. Provide students with the information below and on page 124. Discuss the importance of a balanced diet. Have students create charts that indicate all the foods they eat in one day or over a period of a week. They can write about their chart results and compare their diets to the recommended daily food choices presented in the food pyramid below. (The food pyramid was created by the United States Department of Agriculture in 1992. It shows the kinds of foods and the number of servings needed each day in order to stay healthy.)

It is important that we eat the right amounts and the right kinds of foods every day. That way we keep our bodies healthier and stronger. Study the chart below. It shows the kinds of foods you should eat each day and the number of servings you should have.

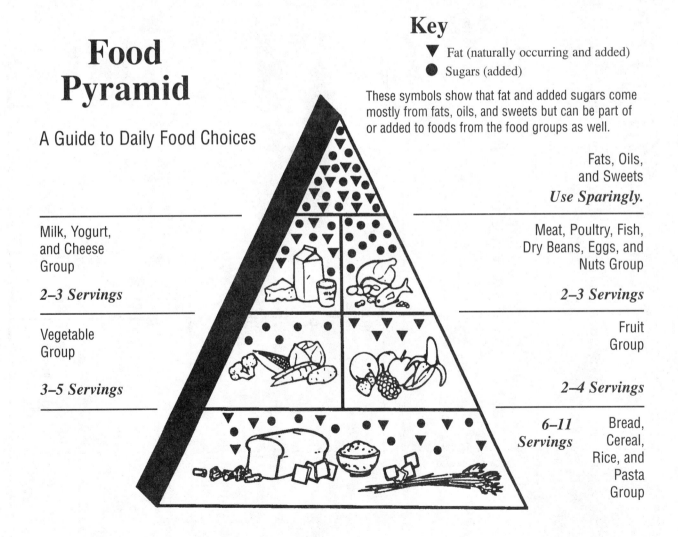

Food Pyramid

A Guide to Daily Food Choices

Key

▼ Fat (naturally occurring and added)

● Sugars (added)

These symbols show that fat and added sugars come mostly from fats, oils, and sweets but can be part of or added to foods from the food groups as well.

Fats, Oils, and Sweets

Use Sparingly.

Milk, Yogurt, and Cheese Group

2–3 Servings

Meat, Poultry, Fish, Dry Beans, Eggs, and Nuts Group

2–3 Servings

Vegetable Group

3–5 Servings

Fruit Group

2–4 Servings

6–11 Servings

Bread, Cereal, Rice, and Pasta Group

Food and Nutrition Activity *(cont.)*

You need to eat so you can have energy to work and play. Eating the right foods helps your body grow and stay healthy. The food ingredients your body needs to stay alive and healthy are called nutrients. This chart shows you how foods and their nutrients help you.

Proteins help build and repair your body. As you grow and need bigger muscles and organs, proteins help to build them. When you scrape and cut yourself, proteins help to repair your skin. Some foods with protein are meat, milk, nuts, beans, and eggs.

Carbohydrates give your body fuel for energy. When you eat carbohydrates you have enough energy to run, work, and play for a long time. There are two types of carbohydrates—starch and sugar. Some foods with starch are bread, cereal, and rice. Fruits with sugar include oranges and apples.

Fats give your body the fuel it needs for energy. Fats do something else, too. The layer of fat under your skin helps keep your body warm. Some foods with fat are cheese and nuts.

Nutrients

Vitamins help you grow and help you use your food. Some vitamins even protect you from disease. Some foods with vitamins are vegetables, whole grain breads, and cereals, nuts, fruit, and eggs.

Minerals help you grow and help you use your food. Minerals also make your blood healthy. Some important minerals are calcium, phosphorus, and iron. Calcium helps your bones and teeth. Phosphorous helps your food get used properly. Iron makes your blood healthy. Some foods with these minerals are milk, eggs, grains, and fish.

Water is not one of the food groups, but you can't live without it. Over half of your body is made of water! Water helps to carry the other nutrients around your body. It helps you digest food and carry waste away. Water also helps keep your body at the right temperature. Almost all foods have water, especially fruits and vegetables.

Inch Rulers

Tools

Make enough copies of this page so that each student will have a six-inch ruler. Reproduce the patterns below onto index or other heavy paper. Cut out the rulers. If you wish to make transparent rulers, reproduce the patterns onto transparency sheets.

Centimeter Rulers

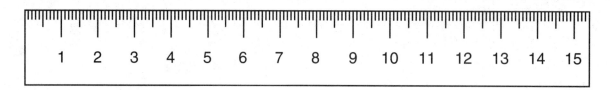

Make enough copies of this page so that each student will have a centimeter ruler. Reproduce the patterns below onto index or other heavy paper. Cut out the centimeter rulers. If you wish to make transparent rulers, reproduce the patterns onto transparency sheets.

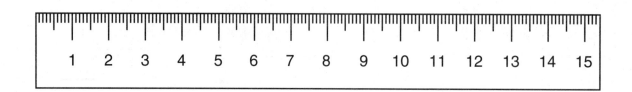

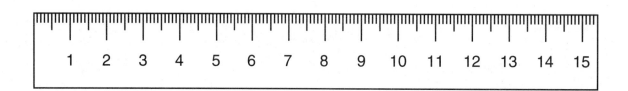

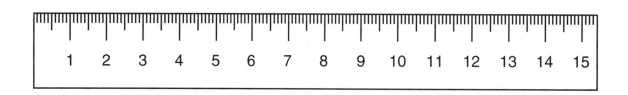

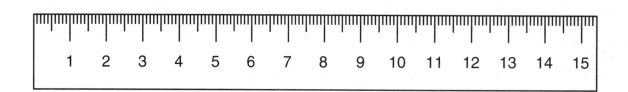

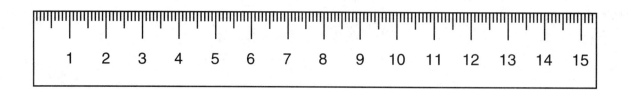

Hundreds Chart

1	2	3	4	5	6	7	8	9	10
11	12	13	14	15	16	17	18	19	20
21	22	23	24	25	26	27	28	29	30
31	32	33	34	35	36	37	38	39	40
41	42	43	44	45	46	47	48	49	50
51	52	53	54	55	56	57	58	59	60
61	62	63	64	65	66	67	68	69	70
71	72	73	74	75	76	77	78	79	80
81	82	83	84	85	86	87	88	89	90
91	92	93	94	95	96	97	98	99	100

Addition Chart

Tools

+	0	1	2	3	4	5	6	7	8	9
0	0	1	2	3	4	5	6	7	8	9
1	1	2	3	4	5	6	7	8	9	10
2	2	3	4	5	6	7	8	9	10	11
3	3	4	5	6	7	8	9	10	11	12
4	4	5	6	7	8	9	10	11	12	13
5	5	6	7	8	9	10	11	12	13	14
6	6	7	8	9	10	11	12	13	14	15
7	7	8	9	10	11	12	13	14	15	16
8	8	9	10	11	12	13	14	15	16	17
9	9	10	11	12	13	14	15	16	17	18

Multiplication Chart

Tools

X	0	1	2	3	4	5	6	7	8	9
0	0	0	0	0	0	0	0	0	0	0
1	0	1	2	3	4	5	6	7	8	9
2	0	2	4	6	8	10	12	14	16	18
3	0	3	6	9	12	15	18	21	24	27
4	0	4	8	12	16	20	24	28	32	36
5	0	5	10	15	20	25	30	35	40	45
6	0	6	12	18	24	30	36	42	48	54
7	0	7	14	21	28	35	42	49	56	63
8	0	8	16	24	32	40	48	56	64	72
9	0	9	18	27	36	45	54	63	72	81

Numbered Bar Graph Form

Tools

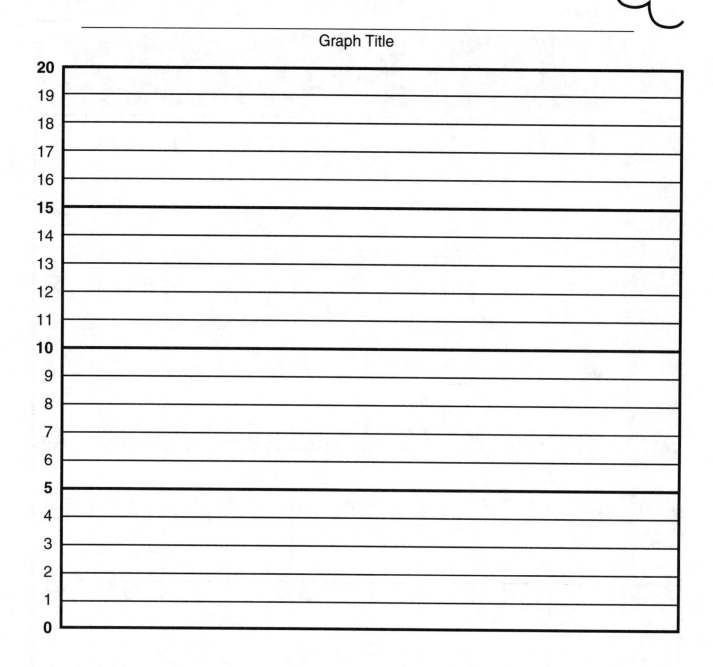

Graph Title

Names of Items

Blank Grid

Clock Pattern

Tools

12
11
1
10
2
9
3
8
4
7
5
6

132

Fraction Blocks

Tools

1

$\frac{1}{2}$	$\frac{1}{2}$

$\frac{1}{3}$	$\frac{1}{3}$	$\frac{1}{3}$

$\frac{1}{4}$	$\frac{1}{4}$	$\frac{1}{4}$	$\frac{1}{4}$

Fraction Blocks *(cont.)*

$\dfrac{1}{5}$	$\dfrac{1}{5}$	$\dfrac{1}{5}$	$\dfrac{1}{5}$	$\dfrac{1}{5}$

$\dfrac{1}{6}$	$\dfrac{1}{6}$	$\dfrac{1}{6}$	$\dfrac{1}{6}$	$\dfrac{1}{6}$	$\dfrac{1}{6}$

$\dfrac{1}{8}$	$\dfrac{1}{8}$	$\dfrac{1}{8}$	$\dfrac{1}{8}$	$\dfrac{1}{8}$	$\dfrac{1}{8}$	$\dfrac{1}{8}$	$\dfrac{1}{8}$

134

Fraction Blocks *(cont.)*

$\dfrac{1}{9}$	$\dfrac{1}{9}$	$\dfrac{1}{9}$	$\dfrac{1}{9}$	$\dfrac{1}{9}$	$\dfrac{1}{9}$	$\dfrac{1}{9}$	$\dfrac{1}{9}$	$\dfrac{1}{9}$

$\dfrac{1}{10}$	$\dfrac{1}{10}$	$\dfrac{1}{10}$	$\dfrac{1}{10}$	$\dfrac{1}{10}$	$\dfrac{1}{10}$	$\dfrac{1}{10}$	$\dfrac{1}{10}$	$\dfrac{1}{10}$	$\dfrac{1}{10}$

$\dfrac{1}{12}$	$\dfrac{1}{12}$	$\dfrac{1}{12}$	$\dfrac{1}{12}$	$\dfrac{1}{12}$	$\dfrac{1}{12}$	$\dfrac{1}{12}$	$\dfrac{1}{12}$	$\dfrac{1}{12}$	$\dfrac{1}{12}$	$\dfrac{1}{12}$	$\dfrac{1}{12}$

Fraction Pies

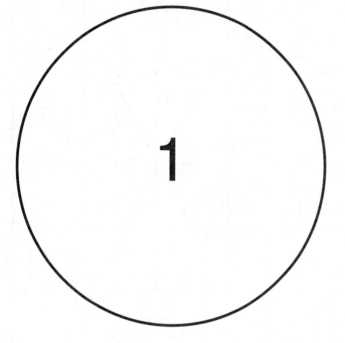

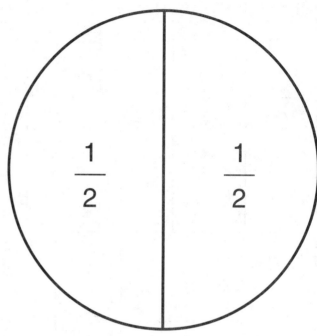

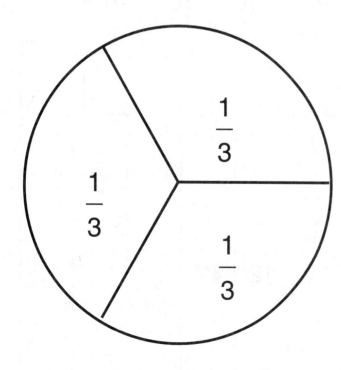

Tools

Fraction Pies (cont.)

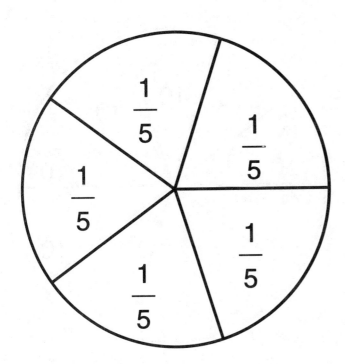

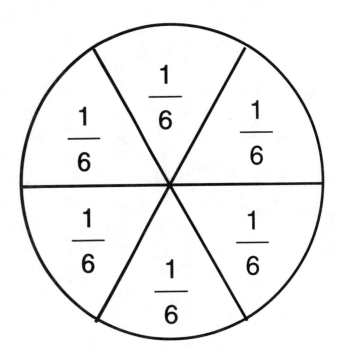

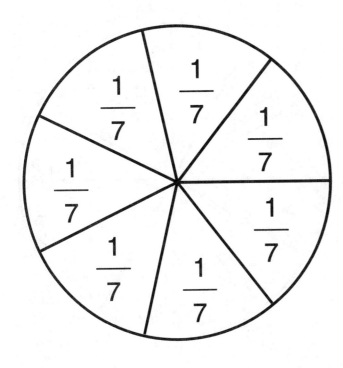

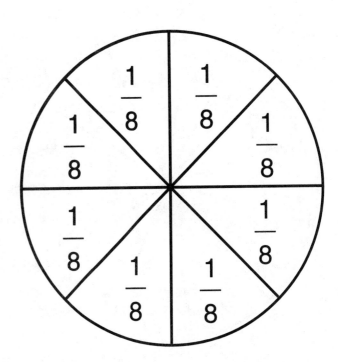

#2323 Math Snacks

Fraction Pies *(cont.)*

Tools

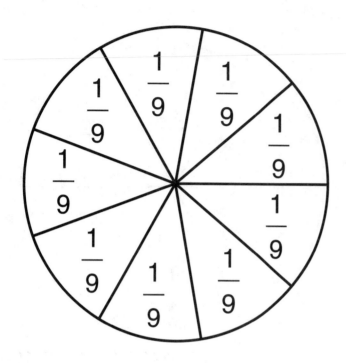

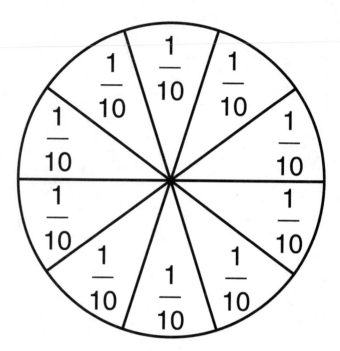

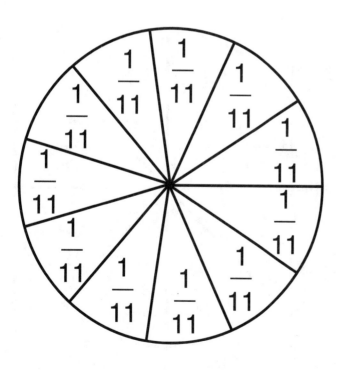

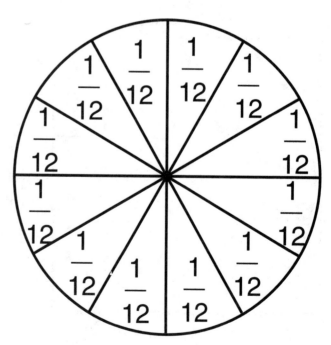

Shape Patterns

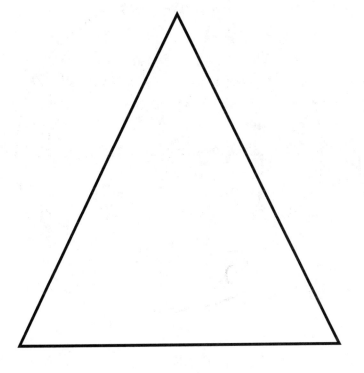

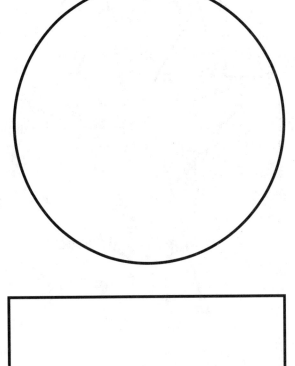

Shape Patterns *(cont.)*

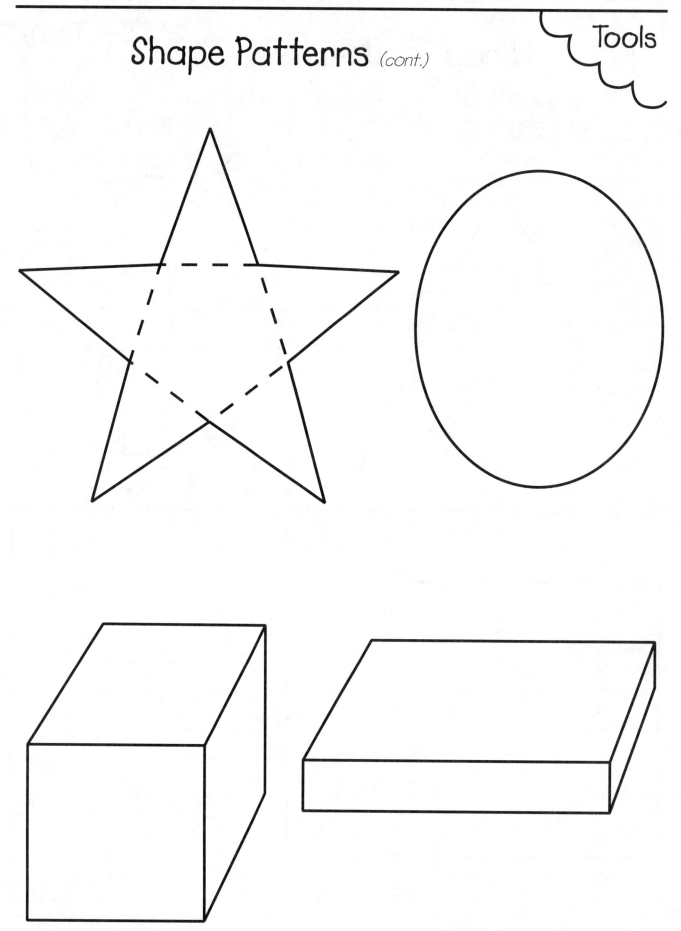

Metric Conversion Chart

	Metric	Customary
Length	1 centimeter (cm) = 10 millimeters (mm) 1 meter (m) = 100 centimeters (cm) 1 kilometer (km) = 1,000 meters (m)	1 foot (ft.) = 12 inches (in.) 1 yard (yd.) = 3 feet (ft.) 1 mile (mi.) = 5,280 feet (ft.) 1 mile (mi.) = 1,760 yards (yd.)
Volume	1 liter (L) = 1,000 milliliters (mL)	1 cup (c.) = 8 ounces (oz.) 1 pint (pt.) = 2 cups (c.) 1 quart (qt.) = 2 pints (pt.) 1 gallon (gal.) = 128 ounces (oz.) 1 gallon (gal.) = 4 quarts (qt.)
Weight	1 gram (g) = 1,000 milligrams (mg) 1 kilogram (kg) = 1,000 grams (g)	1 pound (lb.) = 16 ounces (oz.) 1 ton = 2,000 pounds (lb.)

	*Changing Customary to Metric	*Changing Metric to Customary Length
Length	1 inch = 2.54 centimeters 1 foot = 30 centimeters 1 yard = 0.91 meters 1 mile = 1.6 kilometers	1 centimeter = 0.4 inches 1 meter = 1.09 yards 1 kilometer = 0.62 miles
Volume	1 cup = 240 milliliters 1 pint = 0.47 liters 1 quart = 0.95 liters 1 gallon = 3.79 liters	1 liter = 1.06 quarts 1 liter = 0.26 gallons
Weight	1 ounce = 28.4 grams 1 pound = 0.45 kilograms	1 gram = 0.035 ounces 1 kilogram = 2.21 pounds

* Approximations

Individual Incentive Chart 1

Incentives

Use a favorite stamp or other mark to indicate each activity the student has successfully completed. (Stamp over the activity number completed.) Students can keep these in a math journal or a notebook. If they are comfortable doing so, students can display their incentive charts in the classroom.

1	2	3	4	5	6	7	8	9	10
11	12	13	14	15	16	17	18	19	20
21	22	23	24	25	26	27	28	29	30
31	32	33	34	35	36	37	38	39	40
41	42	43	44	45	46	47	48	49	50
51	52	53	54	55	56	57	58	59	60
61	62	63	64	65	66	67	68	69	70
71	72	73	74	75	76	77	78	79	80
81	82	83	84	85	86	87	88	89	90
91	92	93	H	O	O	R	A	Y	!

Individual Incentive Chart 2

If you complete only a portion of the math snacks activities in this book, use this chart as an alternative to the incentive chart on page 142. Students can work in increments of nine activities to complete a chart. Have students cut off the incentive stamp section at the bottom of the page. Each time the student successfully completes an activity, he or she decorates and cuts out a stamp and then glues it to the chart. Have students write the number of the activity in the box on the stamp.

Name:_____

Decorate and glue a stamp in the chart when you complete an activity.

Student Awards

Congratulations!

_____

is a
Math Snacks
Superstar.

Congratulations!

_____

has successfully eaten
his/her way through
Math Snacks.